Who Broke the Baby?

Who Broke the Baby?

JEAN STAKER GARTON

BETHANY HOUSE PUBLISHERS
Minneapolis, Minnesota 55438
A Division of Bethany Fellowship, Inc.

For information about a video tape entitled WHO BROKE THE BABY? especially geared to teenagers and featuring Jean Garton, please contact:

Tom Talbert Productions, Inc.
6127 Excelsior Blvd.
Minneapolis, MN 55416

Published by Bethany House Publishers
A Division of Bethany Fellowship, Inc.
6820 Auto Club Road, Minneapolis, Minnesota 55438

Printed in the United States of America

Library of Congress Cataloging in Publication Data

Garton, Jean Staker.
  Who broke the baby?

    1. Abortion—Religious aspects.   I.   Title.
HQ766.2.G37   301   79-22683
ISBN 0-87123-608-7

About the Author

Jean Garton, Litt.D., L.H.D., is a resident of Pennsauken, New Jersey, the mother of four children and the wife of a Lutheran clergyman.

Mrs. Garton graduated from Ursinus College with a B.A. in English Literature, did graduate study at Concordia Seminary, Springfield, Illinois, and has been granted an honorary Doctor of Letters (Litt.D.) by Concordia Seminary of St. Louis, Missouri, and an honorary Doctor of Humane Letters (LHD) by Concordia Theological Seminary of Ft. Wayne, Indiana.

A member of the 2.7-million member denomination, The Lutheran Church—Missouri Synod, Dr. Garton serves on that church body's national Board for Public Relations and its national Social Concerns Committee. Her interests and involvement in the area of women's rights and equality led to her election as chairperson of the denomination's Task Force on Women during its four-year existence.

Dr. Garton has represented her denomination's interests by giving testimony before sub-committees of both the United States Senate and House of Representatives during hearings on a Human Life Amendment. She was featured by NBC in a TV special entitled "Alternatives to Abortion" in June 1977.

As a lecturer on numerous topics, Dr. Garton has spoken extensively throughout the United States. She has authored numerous articles which have appeared in periodicals and journals. She has developed and authored a variety of audio-visual materials. At present she is working on a book which examines the role of language in forming public opinion.

Dr. Garton has taught school in grades from kindergarten through the college level. She has been a braille transcriber and teacher of the blind. She was appointed by the New Jersey State Senate to serve on its Committee to Investigate Abortion Clinic Abuses. She was appointed to serve on the Juvenile Conference Committee, a branch of the New Jersey court system, to hear cases of minors with first, second, and third offenses. She is a member of the Board of Directors of American Citizens Concerned for Life and a member of the task force of the Joseph P. Kennedy, Jr. Foundation which researches programs to strengthen the family.

Dr. Garton is co-founder and national president of Lutherans for Life. She was numbered among the "Ten Most Influential Lutherans" in the United States during the year 1978.

Preface

All our children were in bed; the late television news was over, and I was putting the finishing touches to a presentation for medical students scheduled to be given the next day. As I reviewed some slides which might be used, there appeared on the screen a picture of an abortion victim, aged two and one-half months' gestation; her body had been dismembered by a curette, the long-handled knife used in a D & C abortion procedure.

Suddenly I heard, rather than saw, another person near me. At the sound of a sharp intake of breath, I turned to find that my youngest son, then a sleepy, rumpled three-year-old, had unexpectedly and silently entered the room. His small voice was filled with great sadness as he asked, "Who broke the baby?"

How could this small, innocent child see what so many adults cannot see? How could he know instinctively that this which many people carelessly dismiss as tissue or a blob was one in being with him, was like him? In the words of his question he gave humanity to what adults call "fetal matter"; in the tone of his question he mourned what we exalt as a sign of liberation and freedom. With a wisdom which often escapes the learned, he asked in the presence of the evidence before his eyes, "Who broke the baby?"

Why is it that so many of us fail to see and to feel what a three-year-old knows by nature? My personal answer to that question forms the basis for the pages which follow. It explains, in part, the responsibility I feel to speak on behalf of our unborn brothers and sisters. It explains, in part, the commitment I have made to plead their cause. But most of all, it helps explain my faith in God, the God of creation, the God of surprises.

"Life begins at forty!" is a slogan familiar to most of us. Actually, I was looking forward to that time, for I had calculated that finally all the children would be in school and I could start to live my own schedule and pursue my own interests. Birthday number forty came and life began—but it was not mine alone. It included another life, a very "unwanted pregnancy." How unfair! After all those years of bottles and babies, didn't I deserve some freedom? What about my rights and my needs? However, at that time abortion-on-demand had not been legalized by the Supreme Court; so, after much ranting and raving, having no viable choice, I gradually accepted the reality that I was about to become one of those "mature mothers" for whom everyone feels sorry.

My growing feminist interests, plus my inability to

control my reproductive life because of restrictive abortion laws, led me to join a pro-abortion group which was seeking to liberalize the laws of our state. Within weeks after my baby's birth, I was attending meetings and workshops on how to be a pro-abortion activist.

Indoctrination into the language of abortion formed the basis of many of these sessions. "Never accord humanity to what is in the womb," we were told. "Always talk about 'the blob,' never the baby." "Stress the woman's rights and her freedom to choose." However, as time passed, I became increasingly uneasy with such arguments, for it seemed to me they involved a semantic deception which, while effective and persuasive, nevertheless lacked integrity. I decided to develop my own argument, one I could debate with honesty, to support a right-to-abort position.

I spent many months of study and research, examining the issue from various disciplines and perspectives. I read the law, medicine and history. I studied Scripture and the church fathers. I worked long and hard to discover evidence to support my theory. But I found none. I had to either face up to reality and change my position or continue to change reality by disguising the truth. It was then, borrowing the words of C. S. Lewis spoken after he converted to the Christian faith he had set out to discredit, that "I was carried kicking and screaming" into the pro-life position "by the sheer weight of the evidence."

The same catchy abortion slogans which I once employed continue to manipulate the feelings and thoughts of many others. The inaccurate ideas fostered by the abortion rhetoric escape the notice of the less critical. Language is an agent for change and when language lies, when words are warped and twisted perversely, they are eventually emptied of their true meaning. The linguistic deception of the pro-abortion argument "tells it like it isn't."

In those months of study, however, I learned much more about God's wisdom than about the abortion issue. He heard my complaints, displeasure and anger; He received my demands and protests; He bore my weeping and gnashing of teeth—and lovingly endured them all, for He knew exactly what was needed in my life to accomplish His purpose and plan. The unwanted, unplanned pregnancy resulted in a very wanted and loved child. Those who expressed sympathy at my after-forty pregnancy cannot begin to appreciate the special joys and blessings which come to "mature mothers." And life *did* begin at forty for me when I acquired a new and wise teacher in the form of a little boy who taught me what life is really all about.

It was this child who one night slipped in behind me to ask, "Who broke the baby?" By the grace of God, when he is old enough to understand the deeper meaning of his childhood question, I will not have to say that while millions were being destroyed, I was too occupied "seeking a meaningful life" to protest. I will not have to admit that I was too busy "finding myself" to challenge the laws which condoned the destruction. In the "foolishness" of God's plan, His kingdom belongs to children—His little ones whose faith and trust and love are to instruct us. "Who broke the baby?" asks the three-year-old. Because of what you have taught me, my dear son, I pray for the blessing to answer, "Not I."

Contents

1

Seduction by Semantics

The story is told by a young mother of her two little boys, aged four and six, who one day ran into the house and excitedly declared, "We know where babies come from! They come on clouds. Little boys come on blue clouds and little girls come on pink clouds." The mother, having diligently read a number of "how-to" books on child-rearing, felt the time had come to provide her children with some scientific facts; so she sat them down beside her and began to unfold the human story from its beginning.

Using simple language and basic concepts, the young woman skillfully and accurately told of how a baby began with the union of egg and sperm; how both a male and a female were involved in the creation of children and how a baby arrived in this world, not on a cloud, but as a result of the care and protection of the body of a woman which was wonderfully designed for that purpose. What satisfaction she experienced as she viewed their attentive faces! Secure in the knowledge that she had started her children on the road to a mature understanding of the life process, she sent them off to play.

About a year had passed when, one night as she was tucking the boys into bed, they asked, "Mom, do you know where babies come from?"

"Of course, I do," she replied and then with confidence added, "and so do you!"

"Oh, yes, we do," agreed her sons. "Little boys come on blue clouds and little girls come on pink clouds!"

Astonished, the mother realized that they preferred their own version and had chosen to ignore the facts in favor of fantasy. Perhaps it was that they were not intellectually mature enough to comprehend the facts; perhaps they were not emotionally capable of dealing with them; but whatever the reason, theirs was a very human, if childish, way of dealing with truth.

Sometimes adults are just as juvenile as those little boys. Often we, too, use language and distorted images to help us create the kind of reality we want and feel we can accept. For example, consider how our sophisticated but superstitious society deals with the ill-omened number thirteen. Recall being in a tall building, in an elevator going up, watching the floor numbers as they pass by: 9—10—11—12—14—15. . . . Twelve? Fourteen? What happened to the thirteenth floor?

After years of asking that question to groups of teenagers, college students and adults, it has been my experience that in every audience there have been those whose immediate response is, "There isn't any!" I then invite them to consider the alternatives. "Perhaps the steel and mortar terminate after the twelfth floor and are followed by a large area of emptiness above which float all the top floors." The throat-clearing and body language of those present would indicate a discomfort with that explanation, so they would be asked to consider another. "Perhaps there *is* a thirteenth floor, but no one has ever seen it and no one has ever used it. It is a whole floor of top-secret space." While some have not really thought about the subject before, when confronted with the possible options the truth begins to emerge. Of course there is a thirteenth floor. It is a floor where people work or live; a floor with furniture, light and sounds of activity. It is similar to all the other floors of the building, but it makes some people uncomfortable to think about it. They don't want a thirteenth floor to exist, so they call it something else—the fourteenth floor—in order to avoid the reality of its existence.

Such image distortion is part of an unofficial national game we play, tolerated in general because it is viewed as being quite harmless and sometimes humorous. It is neither harmless nor humorous, however, when that kind of distortion is applied to human beings, for this same thought process (or thought-less process) is plaguing our society as it addresses itself to the life-and-death issue of abortion. The unborn child has become the thirteenth floor of the human family.

It makes some people uncomfortable to think

about the preborn infant; they don't want to consider that a person really exists, so they call the infant something else—blob, tissue, product of conception, uterine contents—in order to avoid the reality of his existence. To accept the actuality of the unborn as one like us, a member of the human family, is to admit that this child belongs to us and we to the child. We are then required to admit that what makes us special makes that one special. To accept the reality of the unborn is to immediately recognize a curious resemblance to us; and, thus, eventually we must come to recognize a responsibility for what happens to this little person. *"What"* we decide about the unborn becomes the key moral question.

However, when the United States Supreme Court legalized abortion-on-demand in 1973 (*Roe* v. *Wade*),[1] it changed the question from *what* we decide about abortion to *who* decides, choosing to express its legal decision in ways which violated the use of ordinary language. "Health," for example, was not used to mean "the absence of illness or disease," but rather to encompass the whole state of physical, mental, economic, familial and even social well-being, thereby creating perplexities for society, medicine and law in relation to this crucial issue.

However, to make sound moral choices requires that we use language to describe reality (not create it), to communicate factual information and to aid understanding. As we conclude what may well be catalogued in history as the Sensuous Seventies, we recognize that for an increasing number of people, moral choices are being made on the basis of feelings apart from facts or truth. Ignoring evidence, indeed not even seeking it, many have embraced the maxim of the sensual Frenchman Rousseau who said, "Don't think. It hurts. Just feel." As a result, the decision-making process is not located in the intellect but in the pit of the stomach, in the shifting sands of human emotions. IF IT FEELS GOOD, DO IT! Thus it has become possible for intelligent, educated and religious people to embrace all sorts of illogical absurdities which set aside not only truth but also responsibility for their own actions and for the well-being of others.

Yet that is not a characteristic indigenous to people of this day or place. A story told by Jesus almost 2,000 years ago establishes that the human propensity for ignoring "the facts" is an ageless attribute.

> A certain man went down from Jerusalem to Jericho, and fell among thieves, who stripped him of his raiment, and wounded him, and departed, leaving him half dead.
>
> And by chance there came down a certain priest that way; and when he *saw* him, he passed by on the other side.
>
> And likewise a Levite, when he was at the place, came and *looked* on him, and passed by on the other side.
>
> But a certain Samaritan, as he journeyed, came where he was; and when he *saw* him, he had compassion on him.[2]

Whatever the varied applications of this parable as made by preachers and teachers down through the ages, one point is eminently clear: the three travelers each saw all there was to see, they were each equally provided with the same evidence, but given the facts only one out of three responded to the person in need.

Facts in and of themselves do not serve to convince, for the human mind is never more selective or prejudiced than when it is involved in self-justification. If medical facts were all that is necessary to convince people of a health problem, there would be no cigarette smokers. If legal facts convinced people that certain types of behavior are unacceptable, there would be no criminals. If scriptural facts could of themselves convince people that *God is*, there would be no unbelievers. We tend to create images and realities which affirm our choices and decisions, using language as did the *Alice in Wonderland* character who said, "When I use a word it means just what I choose it to mean."

In George Orwell's visionary book of the future *1984*, a manipulated language called "newspeak" was used to obtain from society the acceptance of ideas and conformity to policies which would be found completely intolerable and immoral if presented in a clearly understood form. That such a practice has a basis in fact and is increasingly being employed in our own society is evidenced by the formation of a national committee to combat it and by the large grants awarded universities to study it.

The Orwellian use, or misuse, of verbal communication has found its way into politics, advertising, government and most successfully into the debate surrounding the abortion issue. Thus we are able to tolerate and even justify the destruction of almost two million preborn human beings each year because, after all, EVERY CHILD SHOULD BE A WANTED CHILD. We can ignore the immediate and long-range effects of such staggering destruction because A FETUS IS NOT A PERSON. Democracy is at stake, we are told, in denying THE RIGHT TO CHOOSE; and the feminist movement sees as essential to liberation A WOMAN'S RIGHT TO CONTROL HER OWN BODY. But what do these phrases really mean? These and others used to promote abortion-on-demand have been repeated so often, visualized on buttons so frequently, advertised on bumper stickers so blatantly that the words are worn smooth and we fail to recognize their absurdity.

Thus it is words, not facts, which shape reality for many people; and Paul's admonition in Ephesians 5:6 is particularly relevant to our situation today, for he warns us to beware of meaningless words which serve to deceive. The distorted images created by the abortion "newspeak" has led us to a form of intellectual suicide from which Paul would rescue us when he urges that we "guard the truth and hold fast to words which are sound." [3] For men and women committed to that Word which has ultimate meaning and truth, it becomes essential that we enter the struggle which demands an honest use of language. We must insist that words and images describe, comprehend and recognize that which *really is* rather than that which is a fantasy manufactured through semantic games which reduce us to intellectual and emotional children. Babies do not come on clouds and, despite current rhetoric, abortion is not merely THE TERMINATION OF PREGNANCY.

2

Every Woman Has a Right to Control Her Own Body

Confucius, the ancient Chinese philosopher, was once asked what he would do to set the world right. After thoughtful consideration he answered: "I would insist on the exact definition of words." Perhaps nowhere is that wisdom more necessary than when one considers the popular phrase, EVERY WOMAN HAS A RIGHT TO CONTROL HER OWN BODY.

As a general principle, such a claim demands a resounding *Amen!* Praise the Lord that through Him, our bodies instead of being "things" have become "temples" with personal rights which free us to choose celibacy or marriage; with legal rights which protect our bodies from exploitation and slavery; and with spiritual rights which allow us to participate as co-creators of life with Him. The status of woman has changed from that of property to person and thus, in a very real sense, every woman *does* have a right to control her own body.[4] However, when that concept is used as a rationalization for abortion, it is essential to examine the meaning of the individual words of that phrase, for then one discovers a gross distortion of the principle.

EVERY WOMAN. Webster's dictionary defines the word "woman" as a "female human being." Since at least fifty percent of those aborted are "female human beings," obviously not "every woman" has a right to control her own body. This slogan advocates elitism for powerful women rather than equality for all women. If the claim that EVERY WOMAN HAS A RIGHT TO CONTROL HER OWN BODY is to have any integrity, it should include all female human beings, all women—even the "little women" in the womb.

HAS THE RIGHT. Legally, no one—man, woman or child—has an absolute right of control over his or her own body. The laws of society, for example, do not permit us to mutilate our bodies or abuse them with drugs. A body which has consumed alcohol is not permitted legally behind the wheel of a car. A body which is covered with chicken pox is not permitted in a classroom. A body which participated in the former craze of "streaking" and ran nude down Main Street found the argument of "the right to control one's own body" ineffective as a defense. Because all of life is interrelated, many individual rights are partial and not absolute.

If such is the reality in the social order, how much

more then should Christians understand that under gospel freedom a woman's rights to her body are not absolute. We are reminded in 1 Corinthians 6:19-20 that our bodies do not belong to us and that we are to use every part of them to give glory back to God because He owns them. Contrast that admonition with the declaration made by women in Rome during a 1976 rally in support of abortion-on-demand: "The body is not to be managed by the doctor and even less by God. The womb is mine and I manage it myself." [5]

Such a blatant statement of independence from the Creator is startling at first reading, but does it not express the essence of an abortion decision regardless of how socially acceptable one's reason might be? Do not abortions, in effect, say to God that He has made a mistake? Such poor timing! Such inept planning! Such incompetent management! We are then faced with the initial temptation of our original parents: take matters into your own hands and you will be like God and know good from evil yourself.[6] To accommodate such a choice perhaps we need to add a clarifying phrase to the familiar hymn: "Take my life and let it be, consecrated, Lord, to Thee." Take my moments and my days, take my hands and feet, my voice and lips—take it all, Lord, but not my womb! There I am God!

Thus, we regard our bodies as flesh, mere meat, mere animal matter and not a prayer to be offered up in thanksgiving. "I appeal to you, I beg you," says Paul, "to make a decisive dedication of your bodies— presenting all your members and faculties—as a living sacrifice, holy and well-pleasing to God, which is your reasonable service and spiritual worship." [7] When abortion is addressed from the perspective of rights, then responsibility *to* Someone and *for* someone tends to get lost in the debate. Responsibility requires us to acknowledge that we are our "brother's keeper," while considering what that means when our "brother" is a fetus.

TO CONTROL. The word "control" means to "exercise authority over; to regulate, curb, restrain." To be in control is to assume responsibility. In recent years responsibility for unborn children has shifted. Before the Supreme Court decision of 1973 (*Roe* v. *Wade*), sexual activity was taken seriously. Both the individuals involved, their families and the community which provided shelters and orphanages, felt a responsibility for the child that might result. Today, with abortion available and employed as an after-the-fact contraceptive, such responsibility is optional. Thus abortion, promoted as a means of being "in control" of one's body, is actually the evidence of a body which has been "out of control."

Most who consent to involvement in sexual activity surely know that despite sex education courses and use of contraceptives, there is the inherent possibility of pregnancy. If one claims to want "control," she must either "curb or restrain" the body before exposing it to the possibility of pregnancy or be responsible for the results of her actions afterwards. "Amidst all the controversy about abortion," said a letter to the editor in a Philadelphia newspaper, "do human beings ever, ever put the emphasis in the right place? It's as though *nobody* ever heard of self-restraint and abstinence." The problem is not that people are hearing about self-restraint and abstinence and acting "as though" they had not heard; the problem is more basic. They have, in many cases, *not* heard. At least I would need to draw that conclusion based on countless sessions in public high schools.

"You owe me an abortion," declared a high school senior during a class discussion. "You" meant all of us who are adults, for she further stated that since she was a minor and since we had not provided her with a foolproof contraceptive, society owed her abortion-on-demand and abortion-paid-in-full.

"What do you mean," I asked, "when you say we have not provided you with any foolproof contraceptive?"

She revealed herself to be a walking manual of contraceptive devices as she launched into a competent presentation of the varied birth control measures and their failure rates. When she finished she said, "See, not one of them is foolproof, so you owe me an abortion; and since I'm a minor, you are responsible for paying for it."

Amid the handclapping and cheers of the other 200 students in the lecture hall, I managed to reply that I didn't *owe* her an abortion; my responsibility to her was to share the truth. "Do you mean to tell me," I asked, "that you are ready to graduate from high school and do not yet know that there *is* a foolproof contraceptive?" Suddenly I had their complete attention! "It is an oral contraceptive," I continued, "and it produces none of the side effects and complications of the pill. It is 100 percent effective: you just open your mouth and say '*no*'!" Later a number of teachers who were present indicated that they were glad I had said that.

"Why haven't *you* been saying that?" I asked.

"Because," they replied, "that would be imposing our morality on them." (To which Paul might have said: "How shall they believe if they have not heard? And how shall they hear without a teacher?")[8]

What have we done to our young people? We have led them to believe that their bodies are machines and that pregnancy is a minor malfunction. But we have neglected to remind them that a machine which is not under supervision, which is allowed to run without restraint, will soon self-destruct.

HER OWN BODY. Since this slogan is used to promote abortion, then the reference to "her own body" is, obviously, to a pregnant body. However, science and medicine will not allow us the luxury of ignoring the evidence that in pregnancy there are two bodies. Regardless of the lack of value we may wish to place on that smaller or newer body, that it exists as a body may be denied only at the sacrifice of intellectual honesty.

The findings of fetologists leave us in no doubt whatsoever that by every physical measurement the intrauterine being is embodied and fully human. The bodies of preborn human beings are able to cry, hiccup, dream, take nourishment and urinate. Early in development the heartbeats can be recorded and brain waves can be detected. The body before birth is one which responds to pain, sucks a thumb, kicks a leg, makes a face and has hands with individual and unique fingerprints. The body of an unborn child would be rejected as foreign tissue from the womb were it not for the placenta, which is not in any woman's body until the fetal child puts it there in the interest of self-preservation! Yet there is more to the pre-birth body than just the physical, for that human being is an entity who can be taught, who has a memory which is operative, and who can distinguish the voice of his or her mother from others around him.

Yet even if we did not have the biological facts to tell us that the prenatal body which exists in pregnancy is a separate human body, we would have to arrive at that conclusion simply on the basis of common sense. All children, both male and female, are carried in the body of a woman. Can *one* body be both male and female at the same time? Many women carry children whose blood differs in type and factor from their own. We know that it is impossible for *one* body to have two different blood types. And what of the child who died while I carried him? He was dead for three days; I was alive. Can *one* body be dead and alive at the same time? A pregnant woman is, literally and accurately, a woman "with child." And that child in the womb is a child whose body is authored and formed by God;[9] a child whose body responds to the presence of God.[10]

In many valid and legitimate ways, every woman does have a right to control her own body; but, while that right is only partial and not absolute, it is above all not unilateral. Abortion, by any logical, biological or theological standard is, at the very least, the destruction of a separate human body.

3

Every Child a Wanted Child

In an old comedy routine, a character is heard to say, "I wants what I wants when I wants it!" to which an off-stage voice responds, "You'll git what you gits when you gits it!" The exchange has become a classic and humorously serves to remind us of the limited control we have over our lives. However, in this era of freedoms and rights, such a concept is intolerable for many. In an age of "doing our own thing," not only do we want what we want when we want it, but we demand that our "wanting" be accepted legally as the justification for previously unacceptable behavior. In the process we have elevated selfishness to the status of a virtue and have developed a social policy which operates on the basis of the seven deadly sins.[11]

Self-gratification and self-indulgence were once

viewed as destructive to humans, both personally and corporately. However, they are embodied in the sentimental-sounding phrase, EVERY CHILD A WANTED CHILD, a phrase which summons up an image that is loving and compassionate. Yet it is neither, for it roots the value of one human being in the desires of another. Children in the womb are thus totally dependent upon the personal "wants" of the individuals who have a vested interest in them. The unborn child must compete with the mother's schedule, job, happiness, convenience and budget and somehow prove that he or she deserves to win over them.

The EVERY-CHILD-A-WANTED-CHILD concept reduces a child to an object. We usually want "things"—a vacation, a raise, a new car or dress. Thus, to "want" or "not to want" children is to dehumanize them. In a consumer-oriented society, we have created an economic system with no room for children. We do not need them for production on the family farm or for old-age insurance. Rather, they have become a costly luxury which, for some men and women, must provide at least as much satisfaction and gratification as the other objects of the "good" life— the yacht, the console stereo, the second car, the color TV. The result is that preborn children are caught in the crunch of competing with objects which mark the classic American success syndrome.

In 1972, prior to the sweeping decision of the United States Supreme Court which legalized abortion-on-demand in every state, a large eastern state was conducting hearings on proposed changes in its abortion laws. Testifying for abortion-on-demand were a clergyman and his wife. He told of his excitement when his wife first informed him that a fourth child was on the way. But, he indicated, she soon convinced him that he was merely on a male ego trip, while she herself wanted an abortion. However, claiming to be democratic about the whole matter and desiring to know what others in the home "wanted," the mother testified that they had gathered together for a family conference. The parents told their three grade-school children that if the pregnancy were allowed to continue, some of them would have to double up in a bedroom, depending on the sex of the new child. The camping trip which they had planned for the summer would most likely have to be cancelled, and surely the bikes they wanted for Christmas would be out of the question. Then they were all given an opportunity to vote. The mother, father and two boys voted for an abortion, but the little girl pleaded for the life of her unborn brother or sister. The majority ruled, of course, and the abortion was carried out. One of the members of the state commission conducting the proceedings asked the mother how she could have denied the pleadings of her daughter to spare the life of the child yet unborn. The mother, totally missing the issue in question, shrugged her shoulders and said, "Well, you can't give your children everything they want."

To "want" a camping trip and a Christmas bike instead of a new brother or sister is made to appear reasonable and logical. Unborn children are having to compete in a smorgasbord of enticing material objects. While many would reject not receiving a new bike as a legitimate reason for aborting a child, they would, on the other hand, defend their own "object" as justifiable—the high school or college diploma, the job promotion, career opportunities or convenient schedules, all of which have become socially acceptable as reasons for aborting an unwanted child.

Yet, EVERY CHILD A WANTED CHILD fails to tell us anything about the child. If I say of you who now share my thoughts: "You are reading," "You are awake," "You are a human," I obviously would be describing you. But when I say, "You are 'wanted' or 'unwanted,' " whom am I describing? Not you! Rather, I would be telling you something about myself, for "wantedness" measures the emotions and the feelings of the "want-er." Thus the Supreme Court decision of 1973, which allows for the elimination of unborn human beings simply because they are not wanted, tells us nothing about the millions who have been destroyed legally since that date, but it does tell us what we have allowed our society to become. The unwanted child is the victim not of his own shortcomings but of those in a society attempting to solve its social, economic and personal problems by the sacrificial offering of its children.

"When a child is unwanted," testified an official representing a mainstream Protestant denomination in 1978, "the most loving thing you can do is abort him." How sad it is that compassion, which once meant "a sympathetic consciousness of another's distress with a desire to alleviate it," has degenerated into a false sentimentality which condones the destruction of human beings as an expression of love. Abortion has become the "good news" for the twentieth century, a form of religious response in which killing is sanctified if we do it for his or her "own good." If the unborn is unwanted, some believe, then prenatal death must surely be preferable to postnatal life! Medical studies indicate that for many women, including those whose pregnancies are planned, the *condition* of pregnancy with its many hormonal and physical changes initially may be unwanted. Yet given the passage of time and supportive counseling, the child of the pregnancy becomes very wanted. On the other hand, reliable and recent studies indicate that the majority of abused children were very wanted as prenatal children but they were "wanted" for the wrong reasons. As use of the pill and abortion have increased, both of which were claimed necessary to eliminate unwanted children, we are left with the incontrovertible fact that after years of legal abortion child abuse has rapidly and steadily increased. Ignorance preserves the stereotype that the unwanted child will become the abused child, who will become the delinquent child, who will become the welfare dependent and/or the criminal. We need to consider that when the value of the unborn child depends upon his or her "wantedness" with its inherent dehumanization, that child then becomes property to be disposed of at the whim or will of the owner. If we view the baby as property while in the womb, it is difficult to adjust that mentality when outside the womb. What we do to him or her becomes a matter of private morality, and laws against child abuse become meaningless. Abortion is the first violence a child can experience at the hands of an adult. It is intrauterine battering and beating, mistreatment and injury once prohibited by law. In fact, a United States Senator, who is also a leading proponent of abortion-on-demand, said publicly he had to admit that the methods used to abort unborn children would qualify, under the laws of his state, as child abuse.

How ironic! For years women have protested being viewed as objects, the property of a male, and thus disposable when inconvenient and unwanted. Now, when womanhood has finally achieved a voice, some are using it to demand, in the same chauvinism which they deplore, a legal right allowing them to dispose of others in the human family when those in their turn become inconvenient and unwanted.

As women increasingly point to the feminine attributes of God, who made both male and female in His image, we are confronted with God as the unconditional lover. He is the One who loves us simply because we are His and not because of what we can do for Him. His love, long exemplified by a parent's love—particularly that of a mother for a child—is a love which serves without its own purposes and motives. However, it is that very attribute which is denied in an aborting society, for then love is dependent on certain subjective criteria. I will love this child *if* he is convenient, *if* he is compatible with my chosen lifestyle, and *if* he contributes to my plans. Yet, perhaps, it is not too unreasonable to claim that of all loves, loving an unborn child whom we cannot see is most like loving God, whom we also cannot see but who exists just as certainly beyond our physical eyes.[12] If we don't "see" the baby before birth, it is not that we lack an active imagination. It is that we lack education, information and faith. If we are in God's image, then ought we not "image" God and be reflectors of a love which views unborn human beings as having an intrinsic value beyond being wanted?

In the *Roe* v. *Wade* and *Doe* v. *Bolton* decisions of 1973, the Supreme Court provided examples of factors which would guide women in concluding that a child was unwanted and, therefore, "abort-able": if the child might "force upon the woman a distressful life or future," if she might be "taxed by child care," if she would experience "embarrassment as a result of being unwed," or if the birth of a child would "deprive a woman of her preferred life style." With such criteria, surely our heavenly Father would have been justified in aborting all of us, for we are not the children He wanted! Surely we distress, tax and embarrass Him! He planned perfect children and we instead are handicapped by sin. He wanted obedient children, while we are rebellious and ungrateful. He designed us as the crown of His creation and instead we have become polluters of the quality of life He desired. We are defective, unacceptable, and according to Paul, an "enemy" [13] of our Father. Surely we are not God's "Children by Choice," to use a pro-abortion slogan. Rather, we are His children by adoption, for there was One who became "distressed, taxed and embarrassed" for us; One who gave up His "preferred life style" for us that we might become sons and daughters of the King, heirs in the family and members of the royal household. Christians ought to be the most vocal defenders of those little ones who are eliminated simply because they are not wanted. Just being alive and alive in Christ places this debt on us!

Wouldn't it be wonderful if there were no unwanted children of any age? No unwanted aged parents by children! No unwanted wives by husbands! No unwanted handicapped, mentally retarded or minorities! No unwanted anybody! But the measure of our humanity, our Christianity, is *not* that there are not unwanted ones among us. Rather, the measure of our humanity, our Christianity, is what we do with those who are unwanted. Shall we care for them, accept them, recognize our oneness with them—or allow them to be killed?

4

Termination of Pregnancy

One day a delegation called on Abraham Lincoln
to demand that he issue an immediate proclamation
of emancipation. The President, knowing that the moment was not opportune, attempted to convince the
group that such a declaration could not be enforced.
The delegation continued in its demand, however, until Mr. Lincoln was led to ask them a question: "How
many legs would a sheep have if you called a tail a
leg?" "Five," they answered. "You are mistaken,"
said the President, "the sheep would still have but
four legs, for calling something a leg doesn't make it
so."

We frequently employ linguistic deception in order
to call something what it is not. A euphemism, for instance, is a pleasant or innocent-sounding phrase used

as a substitute for harsh reality. Euphemistic words or phrases, while less expressive or direct, are also less distasteful and less offensive. The employment of euphemisms proliferated during the Vietnam war, which itself was euphemistically called a "police action." Various phrases were used at that time to allow us to avoid the reality of the killing. "Accidental delivery of ordinance equipment" softened the actuality of shelling our own troops. "Protective reaction" meant to initiate a killing encounter with an enemy; "body count" revealed the number of our troops which the enemy had killed; while "attrition of unfriendly forces" meant the number of the enemy *we* had killed. Perhaps one reason we have become such a violent generation is simply because in practicing the language of deceit we have been able to hide from our own deeds.

TERMINATION OF PREGNANCY is a euphemism which allows us to deal with abortion in the abstract. It is a phrase which disguises the truth, for it implies that abortion is a victimless procedure and thus effectively involves us in verbal beating-around-the-bush. TERMINATION OF PREGNANCY is far more acceptable to one's conscience than "to poison, mutilate or shred preborn babies," words which produce images that brutalize our senses and emotions. That is precisely the purpose of a euphemism, to substitute language whereby we can name things without calling up mental pictures of their reality.

The intent of abortion is the elimination of a small but very real human body in ways which are tolerable because we need not see them with our physical or mental eyes. TERMINATION OF PREGNANCY, as a euphemism for any of the violent procedures which kill unborn children, fails to convey the fact that abortion does not take place upon the body of the woman, although she, obviously, is involved. Indeed, abortion does not take place upon a condition, although the condition—pregnancy—is altered as a result of it. The reality of abortion is that it kills an innocent human being. TERMINATION OF PREGNANCY anesthetizes us to the pain of the action, for clearly it is the life of the unborn child which is terminated.

We further desensitize our perceptions by calling the unborn child a "blob," "a mass of tissue," "fetus" and "embryo." Two women, investigative reporters for a Chicago newspaper, appeared on a nationally televised talk show to present their findings regarding abortion clinic corruption and destruction. While documenting the many unethical, unsanitary and unsafe practices of some legally licensed clinics, the women made clear that they themselves were not opposed to abortion-on-demand. The victims of the abortion procedure, unborn children, were not identified during the hour-long program as anything other than "uterine contents," "birth matter" and "the products of conception." [14] These are phrases which contribute to a depersonalization process so that the destruction of the unborn does not sound like killing. Yet are we not all "products of conception"? Even He who redeemed us, the greatest among us, was "conceived by the Holy Ghost and born of the Virgin Mary." [15] Should not you and I, who *have* been born, more accurately be called "birth matter," rather than those who are aborted and never experience birth? And could not your death or mine be justified on similar linguistic grounds by simply calling us "household contents" rather than "uterine contents"?

If I began a story about an adult, an adolescent and an infant, would you wonder if what was to follow might be an account of the various flowers I grow in my garden or the kinds of cars I have in my garage? Of course not. You would understand that those terms are descriptive of human beings in differing stages of development. So, too, the words "fetus" and "embryo" are scientific terms which tell us where a human being is on life's spectrum. They were never meant to imply that the unborn is somehow sub-human, as some people maintain. Is the adolescent less human than the adult? As tempted as I am to answer affirmatively, having survived a number of teenage children, I must admit that they are *not* less human than adults but merely different in terms of development and dependence. Is the infant less human than the adolescent or merely different in terms of development and dependence? Then is the fetus less human than the infant or merely different in terms of development and dependence?

Does being fully human depend on our size? If so, then surely the Harlem Globetrotters would be more human than most of us. If size determines our humanity, is our humanity diminished when we diet? Does being fully human depend on our physical development? Ossification, the development of our bones, is not completed until we are teenagers; the bodily systems are not fully developed until the mid-twenties; and our mental peak is not reached until we are approximately sixty years of age! Of course, by then, our body has begun to deteriorate, so that from the moment of conception to the moment of death we are constantly in a state of change—physically, mentally, emotionally, psychologically, spiritually—either developing or deteriorating. A human being is not an object or a subject but rather a God-planned project *which begins at conception.*

Does being fully human depend on where we live? It did a few decades ago if one were a Jew who happened to live in Germany. They were the "useless eaters," the Untermenschen or "sub-humans" during the Third Reich. In addition, being fully human did depend on where you lived a few centuries ago if one happened to be a black living on a southern plantation. "The enslaved African race," wrote the United States Supreme Court in its Dred Scott decision of 1857, "are beings of an inferior order and so far inferior that they have no rights which the white man is bound to respect." Today, again, being fully human does depend on where one lives, if where one lives happens to be a womb. In 1973 the Supreme Court removed all legal protection from children who live in a womb and allowed for their destruction by abortion—not for the first three months or for the first six months of pregnancy but, for all practical purposes, until the moment of birth.

The Court said the law need not protect those who are "not persons in the whole sense." What or who is a person in the whole sense? Can one be a person in the half sense? Is the unborn not a person in *any* sense? The Court neglected to tell us. Further, it said that protection need not be granted the unborn until they are "capable of meaningful life." Again the Court left us without a definition of what is "meaningful life."

When the news of the first test-tube baby, Louise Brown, electrified the world on July 25, 1978, Doctors Patrick Steptoe and Robert Edwards said of Louise: "She came out crying her head off . . . a beautiful normal baby." To which Edwards added, "The last time I saw her, she was a beautiful eight-celled embryo." At two days after conception, Louise Brown, unformed, microscopic and nameless, had a meaningful life from her doctor's point of view. Is one human meaningful only if seen by another? What does "meaningful" really mean?

Our individual biological system begins at conception and ends at death, providing us with the obvious fact that life is a continuum. At all stages of this continuum we are human, as the science of genetics can document. Thus our humanity does not depend on our size, stage of development or place of residence, even if society contrarily decides it does by calling the unborn "potentially human."

While in the womb, we may well be a potential infant, a potential teenager and a potential adult, but at all stages we are an actual human being. Birth does not describe a progressive change in a human life but only a change in environment. The change as to the humanity of the unborn takes place in our mind and not in the womb. The terms used throughout Scripture to describe humans in various stages of development document the reality that birth is merely a geographic change rather than a developmental change.

It is significant, for instance, that Luke, a physician, uses but one word, *Brephos*, which means babe in the Greek,[16] to describe a variety of children. John the Baptist, as an unborn child;[17] Jesus wrapped in swaddling clothes as a newborn child;[18] and older children whom Jesus blessed,[19] are all simply "babes." Dr. Luke, medically trained and inspired by the Holy Spirit, makes no distinction between born and unborn children.

Prof. A. W. Liley, Research Professor in Fetal Physiology in Auckland, New Zealand, is known as the "Father of Fetology." As an internationally recognized researcher on life before birth, Dr. Liley pioneered the first successful treatment of the unborn child: the intrauterine blood transfusion. His intimate knowledge of unborn patients has led him to oppose abortion and to make the following comments:

> In a world in which adults control power and purse, the fetus is at a disadvantage being small, naked, nameless and voiceless. He has no one except sympathetic adults to speak up for him and defend him.
>
> Biologically, at no stage can we subscribe to the view that the fetus is a mere appendage of the mother. Genetically, mother and baby are separate individuals from conception. Physiologically, we must accept that the conceptus[20] is, in a very large measure, in charge of the pregnancy.
>
> It is the embryo who stops his mother's periods and makes her womb habitable by developing a placenta and a protective capsule of fluid for himself. He regulates his own amniotic fluid volume and although women speak of their waters breaking or their membranes rupturing, these structures belong to the fetus. And finally, it is the fetus, not the mother, who decides when labor should be initiated.
>
> This, then, is the fetus we know and indeed once were. This is also the fetus whose existence and iden-

tity must be callously ignored or energetically denied by advocates of abortion.[21]

We can call an unborn human a blob; we can label his violent, premeditated death TERMINATION OF PREGNANCY, and we can call a sheep's tail a leg—but calling it something else "doesn't make it so!"

5

Freedom to Choose

In the mid-seventies, some members of a national hockey team had to stand trial for "possession of a weapon dangerous to the public peace." The weapons: their hockey sticks. During the game, each player had the "freedom to choose" how he would swing his hockey stick—forwards or backwards, quickly or slowly—as long as what he "chose" to swing at was a hockey puck. But when one player swung his hockey stick at a spectator and another player swung his at a policeman and subsequently were fined, they came to understand that when exercising the "freedom to choose" they must consider the choice involved.

In the abortion debate one often hears the statement, "Well, I wouldn't have an abortion myself, but I support the right of others to choose." What could be more American and democratic than that? We have convinced ourselves that the "right to choose" is wonderfully patriotic. We would do well, however, to consider the words of Maria Montessori in *The Secret of Childhood*: "We have an instinctive tendency to mask our sins by protestations of lofty and necessary duties, just as in the war a strip of ground dug with trenches or filled with death-dealing devices was camouflaged as a flowering meadow."

When people are frightened and feel helpless, when every traditional structure and institution is challenged, when change is so rapid and far-reaching as to disorient an entire society, it is then that the great seducers present themselves as liberators of the people. At that time people are most vulnerable. The seducer can be an ideology as well as a person, a concept as well as a committee. "Freedom to choose" is semantic seduction, for it is a symptom of a distorted concept of human freedom.

When there is no objective right or wrong, when everyone is simply pursuing his or her own version of what is individually thought to be good, then all acts, all decisions, all choices must be accepted as merely "different" but never immoral or illogical or unacceptable. The "choice" approach to the abortion issue degrades us morally and deceives us spiritually. This will be evident when we apply it to other areas of human rights.

Would we think it wonderfully broadminded if some among us would say, "I wouldn't enslave a black myself, but I support the right of others to choose." Yet there were Americans who did say that and sought support for the slavery system on just those grounds.

Would we think it marvelously tolerant if some among us would say, "I wouldn't send a Jew to the gas chamber myself, but I support the right of others to choose"? Yet there was a whole society of civilized, intelligent people whose seduction by that concept eventually led to the death of over six million Jewish people. Would we think it genuinely liberal if some among us would say, "I wouldn't rape a woman myself, but I support the right of others to choose."

Surely in these related areas of human rights we are able to see that a misapplication of the "freedom to choose" can alter a society's perception of reality. It can create changes in personal and national values which eventually tolerate the institution of slavery, the Nazi holocaust of Jews and the mass extermination of unborn children. Martin Luther once said, "In philosophy a small error in the beginning leads to a very large error at the end. So in theology a small error overturns the whole doctrine." He might well have added that a small error in the concept of freedom distorts the whole system of law.

"I wouldn't have an abortion myself, but I support the right of others to choose." With this position currently being promoted as "the Christian view," we must ask: why would you not have an abortion yourself? If it is a safe procedure, with no serious mental, physical or emotional problems for the woman to consider; if it is not illegal or immoral; if it is not killing a human being or an offense against society, then why ever would *you* not have an abortion? However, if you would not because it is unsafe for the woman, immoral as social policy or deliberately destructive of an innocent human life, then how can you legitimize and bless the choice of others to do so?

As citizens in a democratic society, as people who are admonished to be our brother's keeper, we must not surrender to the illusion that we are responsible only for what we ourselves do. We must come to see that we are also, and always, responsible for what we allow to be done. Having jumped on a cultural bandwagon which assures a person that "I'm OK, you're OK," many have absorbed an assembly-line type of morality in which each accepts a limited area of responsibility but feels insulated from overall accountability.

As the shock waves from the 1978 mass suicide of 900 members of the People's Temple in Guyana circled the globe, many connected with that settlement were questioned and interviewed. "How does it feel," a reporter asked a member of the community's legal staff, "that you were involved in this grotesque thing?" "Well," responded the attorney, "I don't take any personal responsibility for it. . . . The fact that they fizzled out at the end doesn't take away the years of affirmative works they had done." "They didn't 'fizzle out' at the end!" exclaimed the incredulous interviewer. "They killed babies!"

When we tolerate abortion-on-demand on the grounds of "freedom to choose," we, in effect, favor the right of each individual to impose his or her morality on the most defenseless in the human family. Abortion then, for all practical purposes, becomes another spectator event for which we do not take personal responsibility.

Those who insist on euphemistically being called "pro-choice" have stated periodically and publicly that they do not view abortion as "a good solution" but rather as "a last resort in birth control." Yet, strangely, it is right-to-abort individuals and organizations which oppose legislation which would insure "informed consent," which is the pillar of free choice. We can hardly rejoice in a woman's so-called "freedom to choose" when she is informationally deprived and medically manipulated. To hinder the dissemination of information which relates to the decision-making process is indefensible if we are to credit women with intelligence. Further, such denial of information places women in a position of being victimized by their own sexuality and by those who would profit from it, either personally or economically.

A clergyman, publicly debating in support of a woman's "right to choose," was asked if in his counseling he informed women of the nature of the life which they were carrying or the risks to which they were subjecting themselves in the abortion procedure. He indicated that imparting such information would tend to instill fear and guilt in women and amounted to harassment. In effect, such a position as his implies that "it is for their own good" that women blindly trust those who not only have great power to influence their choices but who also will eventually profit financially from it. Yet, information directs and programs activity. Information is essential if genuine "freedom to choose" is to be a reality. St. Paul recognizes this when he prays that the love of God's people "will keep on growing more and more, together with true knowledge . . . so that [we] will be able to choose what is best." [22]

There is a further consideration, one which concerns the difference between the freedom to choose and the right to choose. It is the age-old Genesis dilemma of Adam and Eve. Surely they had the "freedom to choose" to eat of the forbidden tree. But in exercising their freedom to do so, they chose to ignore the reality that they did not have the *"right* to choose" to eat of it, for it had been forbidden by God. Freedom is not the liberty to do what we want to do but to do what we must—what God determines, directs and demands. If we perceive this statement as restrictive, confining, we would do well to remember the Apostle Paul's lavish use of such a concept in his epistles. Having freely chosen to obey God rather than man, he testifies to living a liberated life of great joy.

In actuality, to be opposed to abortion-on-demand is truly to support the "freedom to choose," for it recognizes:

—the right of fathers to choose to save their unborn children from destruction, a right now denied by Supreme Court Decision;[23]

—the right of taxpayers to choose not to fund the abortion procedure as now required by many states;

—the right of parents to choose to be involved in an abortion decision made by a minor daughter, a right now prohibited by the Supreme Court decision of July 1, 1976;

—the right of unborn children to live.

"I wouldn't have an abortion myself, but I support the right of others to choose." Period. We end the sentence without completing the thought. We must ask . . . to choose *what*? God identifies the choice for us.

"I call heaven and earth to record this day against you, that I have set before you life and death, blessing and cursing; therefore, *choose life* that both you and your seed may live." [24]

6

A Fetus Is Not a Person

"What's this I hear about you throwing Linus out of the house?" Charlie Brown asked Lucy in a segment of the Peanuts cartoon strip. "That's not legal, you know. Legally, you can't throw him out."

"Oh, yes, I can and I did," replied crabby Lucy. "Legally a big sister can throw out a younger brother because she's bigger than he is and because he *bugs* her all the time. She can do it and I did it, and if you're smart, Charlie Brown, you won't get involved."

To which an intimidated Charlie Brown responded, "I'm very smart."

Webster's dictionary defines the word "bug" as meaning "to irritate, to annoy." When we use the phrase "bug off," we are saying in effect, "Get out of here. You're not wanted." On January 22, 1973, by

Supreme Court ruling, the crabby Lucy philosophy became the law of the land and we can now eliminate those in the human family who are smaller than we are simply because they "bug" us. We are permitted to "throw out" a younger brother or sister from our societal house, the human family in which we all live, and we may do it legally and permanently. Thus, almost two million preborn children are destroyed each year because their presence in the family "bugs" someone.

Yet such a policy is in conflict with this nation's historical precedent. Beginning in 1827 with the discovery of the nature of conception, each state (and eventually the national government through the passage of the Assimilative Crimes Statute of 1866) responded with strict laws to protect the life of a preborn human being. Further legislation granted the fetal child such fundamental rights as the right to collect damages for injuries suffered before birth, the right to blood transfusions while in the womb (despite the religious objection of the parents) and the right to inherit property or to be a beneficiary of a trust. Until 1966 every state prohibited abortion except when the life of the mother was endangered.

The passage of such laws was clearly in keeping with the principle established by the Declaration of Independence which states that all men are created (not born) equal and are endowed by their Creator with certain inalienable rights, the first of which is *life*. However, in 1973 a woman's "right to privacy," her right to say "bug off" to an unborn child, became absolute.[25] It superseded the inalienable right to life with which all humans have been endowed by the

Creator and which had been recognized in this nation's foundational document.

The arguments which led to that change in law and in the growing public acceptance of abortion moved through various stages. In the early sixties, those seeking liberalized laws first employed the following theories:

—*The Tissue Theory*, which said that what is in the womb is merely a blob, tissue, part of a woman like a tonsil or appendix. "Not so," protested the geneticists. The evidence was conclusive that what develops in the womb is genetically different from the mother and, indeed, from every other human being which has ever existed. These facts forced the argument to:

—*The Parasite Theory*. This position admitted that while what is in the womb is genetically different from its mother, it is, nevertheless, a parasite. "Not so," responded the biologists. A parasite is an organism of one species living upon a different species; in pregnancy there is a dependent relationship within the same species. A parasite, invading from the outside, usually remains for the life of the host and often damages that host. In pregnancy the child associates with the mother in a normally healthful manner and in a temporary relationship. Such facts, easily found in any biology textbook, moved the pro-abortionists next to argue:

—*The Life Theory*, in which it was finally admitted that what is in the womb is, of course, human life—genetically and biologically—but it is not a human *being*. "Not so," replied the fetologists. What is in the womb is a patient; a human being who can be treated, transfused, examined and x-rayed.

The evidence from so many branches of science and medicine could not be ignored. As accurate information reached the general public, the previous arguments were abandoned as untenable. Currently the argument is expressed in the phrase A FETUS IS NOT A PERSON.

What is a "person"? "Person" is a legal term, not a scientific one. Not all "persons" are people. Trade unions and oceangoing vessels can be "persons." Corporations, for instance, bring into being entities which did not exist before. As such, they have an identity and acquire legal personhood. Their property rights are protected by law. The law insures their freedom to operate without fear of confiscation. Only those who are legal persons are granted the protection of the law. Legal personhood is the way our society declares that an entity, human or otherwise, is of value and thus deserving of rights under the law.

By placing unborn human beings *outside* the protection of the law, it became possible to deny them basic rights. This is not the first time in our history that we have made a distinction between the biological category of living human beings and the legal concept of "person." At one time in our history American Indians were not legal persons because we did not grant them the protection of our Constitution. Thus we were able to take by force anything which belonged to them. Usually what we wanted was their land, so we denied them the right to property. Next in our national list of non-persons were black slaves, declared to be chattel and property of their masters as a result of the Dred Scott decision of 1857. What we wanted from slaves was their labor, and so we denied them the right to liberty. We now rightly view this period of our history with shame, but we must remember that slavery then, as abortion now, was a very profitable practice which was accepted socially, condoned by many churches of the day and held as legal by the United States Supreme Court.

In 1973, another group of human beings were added to the non-person list: the unborn. If we want their space in this world, their portion of food, share of resources, part of the budget or if we just simply *do not* want them, we can deny them their right to life.

> Unborn human beings denied LIFE.
> Black human beings denied LIBERTY.
> Indian human beings denied PROPERTY.

Our Constitution declares that "No state shall deprive any person of life, liberty or property without due process of law." Yet, in fact, we have denied all three for the sake of convenience, economics and expediency. History has proven us wrong about the Indians. History has proven us wrong about the blacks. We cannot afford to wait for history to prove us wrong about the unborn.

Denying the unborn personhood has no basis in Scripture. In the many references in the Bible to children, both born and unborn, never is the child mentioned in anything other than a personal sense. "The Lord called *me* from the womb," says Isaiah.[26] To Jeremiah He said, "Before I formed *you* in the womb I knew *you*. Before *you* were born I consecrated *you* and appointed *you* to be a prophet." [27] Paul said that God "set *me* apart before *I* was born." [28] In Psalm 139:13-16 God's care and all-pervasive presence and involvement in each individual life from the moment of conception is expressed: "Thou hast covered *me* in *my* mother's womb. *My* substance was not hid from thee, when *I* was made in secret."

Psalm 51:5 is translated to read, "You know I was born guilty, a sinner from the moment of conception." [29] David is declaring that he, as all mankind, possessed a fallen nature that would later be characterized by sin. Can human sin exist apart from a human person? Christ's death for all sinners is witness to the fact that each of us is a person so valuable, so important and so special that we are worth the life of God himself.

If personhood is bestowed by society on only those entities it views as valuable and if, as history has shown, society is changeable in its judgments, which class of human beings might next be given the status of non-person?

7

Eliminate the Back Alley:
Legalize Abortion

Forty years ago a photographer for *Life* magazine
was in the British colony of Singapore filming a story.
While there he became intrigued by an unusual aspect
of governmental operation, an official opium industry.
Having been unable to stop the use of opium completely, British colonial administrators had issued li-
censes to confirmed addicts which permitted them to
buy a regular supply cheaply. To insure that the drug
met quality standards, the government set up a special factory complete with machinery and white-
uniformed handlers. If people were going to use
opium, despite laws against it, then seemingly the
only reasonable course was to insure that its use was
made as safe and sanitary as possible. Nevertheless,

Life magazine in a subsequent picture story on the government-run opium factory noted that, despite the modern equipment and hygenic operation, "the end result was the same as ever." [30] The same problems arose, the same physical and emotional effects appeared, and the same destruction of human potential and human life resulted.

Similarly, one of the most commonly heard arguments for legal abortion is that women have always had abortions and always will, despite laws against the practice. Therefore, as a humane civilization, shouldn't we insure their safety and protection by legalizing the procedure? It is certainly true that abortions have always occurred regardless of laws to the contrary. However, guaranteeing women's safety and protection by legalizing the procedure needs to be examined closely.

The problem of abortion is not a by-product of contemporary society. Abortive practices have been recorded for 3,000 years and history has documented the negative effects on various civilizations when abortion became part of the social policy. Aristotle, Plato and Hippocrates all made references to such practices, noting the use of abortion as "a means of controlling the population." Historians have observed that such policies among pagan societies invariably led to a death rate larger than the birth rate. Much of Athens' loss of freedom and the eventual fall of the Greek empire have been attributed to a gradual decrease in its population. Ploybius, writing in approximately 150 B.C., stated that "the whole of Greece has been subject to a low birth rate . . . owing to which cities have become deserted." Augustus Caesar, the

Roman emperor, observed that "women who wanted to be sexually rather than maternally beautiful" were commonplace. "The desire for individual freedom," he complained, "seems to be running counter to the needs of the race." [31]

There is no doubt that abortion always has been and always will be part of history as long as humans exist. In every generation, every society, every community, the children of Cain will be found. For Cain, the world was overpopulated as long as Abel was in it. Abel "interfered with his preferred life-style" and diminished "the quality of life" Cain desired. For some people the solution then, now, and always will be the elimination of the unwanted one.

Yet while abortion remains a reality we need to examine the premises which underlie the appeal to legalization. Does decriminalization of abortion actually eliminate problems or are we merely indulging in wishful thinking? Is an appeal to legalization medically and socially sound? Those who would respond affirmatively to this question do so on the basis of four assertions.

> *Premise #1*—Since laws against abortion have always been disregarded by women, they should be removed.

In this country a vehicle is stolen every 32 seconds. Should we legalize car theft since one million cars will be stolen each year despite laws against it? One hundred twenty-four million shoplifting incidents occur each year and cost American business ten million dollars a day.[32] Some teenagers do not view shoplifting as a crime but as part of a "beat-the-system" game. Consequently, the highest percentage of shop-lifting offenses are committed by teens. Should we, therefore, legalize shoplifting since so many arrested do not believe they are doing anything wrong? Since most muggings occur at night on back streets, should we eliminate illegal back alley muggings by legalizing them from 9 to 5 on Main Street? *Because laws are broken, is that justification for eliminating them?*

Premise #2—Legalizing abortion will eliminate back-alley abortions.

It can be shown statistically that in contemporary countries where abortion has been legalized, there was an initial decrease in criminal abortions; *but the level of such activity eventually reached that of legal abortion and sometimes surpassed it.* Dr. Christopher Tietze, the world authority on the statistics of abortion, reported that "although one of the major goals of the liberalization of abortion laws in Scandinavia was to reduce the incidence of illegal abortion, this was not accomplished. Rather, as we know from a variety of sources, both criminal and legal abortions increased." [33] A U.S. Public Health report stated that "in Hungary, though there are more legal abortions than live births, illegal abortions have not decreased. . . . In East Germany, illegal abortions as well as births and pregnancies increased between 1948 and 1950, a period in which the abortion laws were liberalized to allow abortions on social as well as on medical grounds. . . . From 1946-56, illegal abortions rose more than legal abortions." [34] In England, according to a member of parliament, the liberalized abortion law enacted in 1966 "produced increasing deaths of patients and a growing number of abortion mills. Back-street abortionists, instead of decreasing, have increased." [35] In states such as Colorado and New York, which liberalized their laws before the national ruling of 1973, official sources reported a similar situation. In Colorado, said the director of the state's health department, "the liberalized abortion law of 1968 has not done what we hoped it would do—it has not cut down the percentage of illegal abortions." [36] The chief medical examiner of New York was "most concerned" about the illegal abortions still being performed there. "We're still getting abortions like those we had prior to liberalization of the law. . . . " [37]

We are naive to think that all those who risked fines, jail and social disgrace to perform abortions when they were illegal would voluntarily abandon their practice now that abortions are legal and are accepted as a supposed social good. Experience and honesty tell us that we have a tendency to use our intellects not to arrive at the truth, but to support the presuppositions and prejudices with which we began. In this matter our minds may lead us to *assume* that back-alley abortions disappear after legalization, but when human life is at stake, it is required of us "to examine everything carefully," "to test everything." [38]

Premise #3—Legalizing abortion will provide safe abortions.

The fact that a physician performs the abortion procedure does not mean that it is health-producing or health-maintaining. It underscores the fact that the procedure carries risks. Even under the best conditions there are dangers inherent in an abortion regardless of where or by whom it is performed.

Time magazine, in its report of the 1978 Chicago exposé of abortion clinics, made the following observations:

> The investigators charged that the Illinois department of public health, which is supposed to license and inspect abortion clinics, is so careless that at least two clinics were permitted to operate without valid licenses. And state officials were apparently unaware that twelve women have died after clinic abortions in that state since 1973, when the operations were legalized.[39]

The short- and long-range complications for women undergoing legal abortion whether in hospitals or clinics, as well as the effects on subsequent pregnancies and reproductive functions, have been documented by numerous countries and, most recently, by the National Institute of Child Health and Human Development.[40] The mounting statistics of hemorrhaging, infection, perforated uterus, cervical damage, sterility and death as well as the increased incidence of malpractice suits related to abortion indicate that *legal abortions are not necessarily safe for women.* Certainly a legal abortion is no safer for the unborn child than is an illegal one.

For whom, then, *is* legal abortion safe? Perhaps only for the back-alley abortionist. Pamela Zekman, investigative reporter for the Chicago *Sun-Times*, summed up her research by stating: "In 1973 the Supreme Court legalized abortion. As it turns out, what they legalized in some clinics in Chicago is the highly profitable and very dangerous back-room abortion." [41]

Premise #4—The reason abortion was illegal in the past was not out of concern for the fetus. A lack of medical skills and the absence of medication made the procedure unsafe for women. Modern techniques and medicines have minimized the risks; therefore, it is no longer necessary to prohibit it by law.

Such a premise will not bear the scrutiny of history. It was not until the early 1800's that science unraveled the nature of conception. With the astounding revelation that a separate and totally unique individual life began with the union of an egg and sperm, physicians began to address themselves to the matter of abortion. In 1857 a committee of doctors was appointed by the American Medical Association to investigate the matter. That committee submitted its findings at the Twelfth Annual Meeting of the AMA held in Louisville, Kentucky, in 1859. The committee reported that the reasons people resorted to abortion stemmed, first, from—

> "a widespread popular ignorance of the true nature of the crime—a belief even among mothers themselves that the fetus is not alive till after the period of quickening . . . and, secondly, from the grave defects of our laws as regards the independent and actual existence of the child before birth, as a living being." [42]

Such errors, the committee stated, were based on "mistaken and exploded medical dogmas."

> Our duty is plain. . . . As a profession we are unanimous in our condemnation of the crime. . . . It is our duty as physicians, both publicly and privately, to enlighten this ignorance. If the tenets of the law, here unscientific, unjust, inhuman, can be bettered

... if these great, fundamental and fatal faults of the law are owing to doctrinal errors of the profession in a former age, it devolves upon us . . . to see these errors removed and their grievous results abated.

In accordance, therefore, with the facts in the case, the committee would advise that this body [the AMA] . . . publicly express its abhorrence of the unnatural and now rapidly increasing crime of abortion; that it avow its true nature, as no simple offence against public morality and decency, no mere misdemeanor, no attempt upon the life of the mother, but the wanton and murderous destruction of her child;

And that the Association recommend, by memorial, to the governors and legislatures of the several states, and to the President and Congress, a careful examination and revision of the law as it relates to this crime.[43]

On May 3, 1859, the American Medical Association unanimously adopted the resolution prepared by the Committee which condemned "the act of producing abortion, at every period of gestation, except as necessary for preserving the life of either mother or child" and encouraged the various state medical societies to urge the legislatures to strengthen the laws against abortion.

This the state societies and individual doctors did; consequently, when in 1866 the Congress of the United States adopted the Assimilative Crimes Statute, included were strong state anti-abortion laws. Two years later the same men who had adopted the Assimilative Crimes Statute also affirmed the Fourteenth Amendment to the Constitution. This amendment stated that "no state shall deprive any person of life, liberty or property without due process of law, nor deny to any person the equal protection of the law." Yet it was in this Amendment that the Supreme Court in 1973 found an implied "right-to-privacy" which gave women the liberty to procure an abortion at any time in the course of pregnancy. It was this same Amendment which the Court used as the basis for its ruling which made invalid all the existing state abortion laws. At the time of the passage of the Fourteenth Amendment, none of the existing anti-abortion laws were even challenged, much less struck down. There is no historical evidence to indicate that those who had framed the Fourteenth Amendment or the Congress which proposed it or the states which eventually ratified it ever intended it to legitimize or legalize abortion.

What a strange situation now exists: laws abolished because they are broken; legalization which produces increased numbers of abortions but not necessarily safer ones; back-alley operations legitimized and a disregard for testimony from medical history.

As we view the utilitarian, pragmatic arguments for the legalization of abortion, we need to recognize that a society as well as individuals within it often possess blind spots in the matters of right and justice. Some today applaud the present situation and have summed up recent legal changes in the words of the popular phrase, "We've come a long way, Baby." Yet perhaps all that is really demonstrated is that progress, as beauty, is in the eyes of the beholder.

8

Abortion Is a Catholic Issue

During a presentation on abortion before a class of college students, I was interrupted by one of the young men present who said, "Listen, lady, we don't want your Catholic morality forced down our throats!"

"Oh, but I'm not Catholic," I replied.

"Well, what are you?" he asked.

"Lutheran," I responded, to which he countered, "Well, that's the same thing!"

Such a comment by a seemingly intelligent person causes one to wonder what would lead him to that conclusion. Was he uninformed, lacking in knowledge? Was it a tactic whereby he could "cop-out" on the main issue by diverting the discussion elsewhere? Or was he merely demonstrating an unwillingness to acknowledge facts which conflicted with his own preconceived notions and personal prejudices? All of these could explain the eagerness with which some claim that ABORTION IS A CATHOLIC ISSUE.

Those who are *uninformed* are experiencing the void caused by a negligence from the media to report on non-Catholic involvement in the pro-life movement. As a result, many Protestants and Jews have been written out of the script and are without a public voice or identity on the abortion issue. Those who would *"cop-out,"* by shifting the emphasis of the discussion to a religious perspective, do so in order to avoid coming to grips with the fact that our society has legalized private killing. Those who are *unwilling* to adjust their presuppositions in light of the evidence merely demonstrate the cleverness of the human mind which is never more resourceful than when it is engaged in self-vindication.

It has become popular to caricature those who protest the current abortion laws as Catholic. The prevalence of that concept is illustrated by the following episode. Two United States congressmen, nationally identified for their pro-life voting records, were the subject of a mail investigation by the American Civil Liberties Union. The ACLU attorneys argued that legislation supported by these men represented the moral viewpoint of only one denomination—Roman Catholic. A sociologist had provided the ACLU attorneys with key words which, if they appeared in the incoming or outgoing mail, were supposed to indicate a "Catholic bias." The list included the words "God," "right to life," and "unborn child." [44] Undoubtedly, on that basis Catholics and Lutherans *are* "the same thing." Then of course so are Baptists, Methodists,

Jews, agnostics and many others who use such language.

The sectarian scenario changes, however, depending on the geographical location of the discussion. In the northeast corridor of the country, abortion opposition is pictured as a Catholic effort; in the south it is identified as an evangelical crusade, and in Utah as a Mormon pressure group. Yet, in January 1979, *Time* magazine reported that "Poll data indicate[s] that about half the population agrees with the Catholic belief that human life begins at conception, and that only a minority of Americans are as liberal as the Supreme Court regarding abortion on request." [45]

The attempt to place a label of sectarian bias on those opposed to abortion veils the facts, for neither church history nor secular history will support the claim that ABORTION IS A CATHOLIC ISSUE. While it is true that the Roman church has taken a forceful stand on abortion, additional data will furnish a more complete picture.

American history records that the strong anti-abortion laws which were passed in this country during the mid-1800's were enacted by Protestants. Roman Catholics had little influence in such areas due to their lack of numbers and to restrictions placed on their participation in the political process. Until the Supreme Court decision of 1973, 47 states had laws against abortion, yet Catholics are not a religious majority in more than one or two of those. Of the 13 Senate co-sponsors of a 1974 constitutional amendment which sought to protect the life of the unborn, only one of the co-sponsors was a member of the Roman Catholic Church. Further, it appears that there was only one Catholic signer of our Declaration of Independence, the document which endorsed a "theology" affirming that " . . . all men are created equal, that they are endowed by their creator with certain inalienable rights; that among these are life. . . . "

Church history reveals that opposition to abortion dates back to the beginnings of the Christian community. Early church writings such as the Didache, written about 80 A.D., took a strong stand against both abortion and infanticide. This position has prevailed throughout the centuries to current times. "Every major Protestant theologian," said Harold O. J. Brown, professor of theology at Trinity Evangelical Divinity School, "from John Calvin, in the days of the Reformation, through Dietrich Bonhoeffer, whom the Nazis killed, through Francis Schaeffer, today, is strongly anti-abortion." To those names could be added Ramsey, Williams, Outler, Barth, Thielecke and many others who represent non-Catholic religious positions.

Contemporary history demonstrates that the most restrictive abortion laws are found in European Communist countries which, having experienced liberalized abortion for many years, have found that it weakened them militarily, reduced their labor force and affected the health of their women as well as the children born subsequently. Current attempts by numerous countries to further restrict abortions are rooted not in religious bias but in very pragmatic considerations. Prof. T. S. Ueno of Tokyo's Nihon University, speaking to the Ninth Congress of the International Academy of Legal and Social Medicine, observed that his country's liberal abortion policy has had some unfortunate consequences. He noted that abortion has replaced contraception and that Japan now has too few young people to care for the growing proportion of its population over 65. "Abortion has become a way of life," he said. "Moral life has become disorderly. It is an age of free sex, and the life of the unborn is not respected. We can now say the law is a bad one." [47]

Religious and non-religious people alike object to abortion not because they belong to a particular organized religion but because, for a variety of reasons, they believe it uncivilized to kill one human being at the request of another. The fact that some have religious convictions does not make abortion a religious issue. In the 1800's many of the leading abolitionists were clergymen. That did not make abolition a religious issue. The highly visible and vocal involvement of Catholic priests, nuns and bishops in matters of civil rights, Vietnam and food stamp programs did not make those Catholic issues.

Those who adhere to the Judeo-Christian ethic concerning the sanctity of all life do so on the basis of four principles:

(1) that life is a gift from God;
(2) that human beings are created for eternal life;
(3) that human life is created for fulfillment;
(4) that life and death belong in the realm of God's providence.

Certainly these points of emphasis are not uniquely Roman Catholic but have been shared by people of various religious persuasions for many centuries. Departure from strong objection to abortion is a phenomenon of recent date. Historically, it is an abandonment of principles traditionally held in common by both Christians and Jews.

Such abdication brings to mind the comments of Dr. Peter Berger, noted professor of sociology at Rutgers University, who stated that mainstream Protestantism and much of contemporary Judaism have been characterized by "a monumental failure of nerve." He argues that in an attempt to become more "relevant" men and women of religion have accommodated themselves to a secularized culture, providing a dramatic illustration, in his words, "of the blind leading the blind." [48]

Perhaps nowhere has the capitulation to secularism been as evident or as rapid as in the matter of abortion, which finds some church leaders not only repudiating their own historical position but also attacking those who have remained faithful to it.

In October of 1977 approximately 200 Protestant and Jewish church leaders, supporting abortion-on-demand, issued a statement entitled, "A Call to Concern," which specifically singled out the Roman Catholic involvement on this issue. Describing those who opposed abortion-on-demand as "extreme," "blind" and "dangerous," they characterized their own position in support of abortion as "moral," "responsible," "sound" and "rooted in deeply held convictions." [49] Those who signed the document contended that women are entitled to abortion. They, thereby, ruled out the possibility that unborn children are persons deserving of protection from the state. Having taken that position, they were asking society to accept with them an important statement of a moral nature, one which *diminished* the value of preborn life. Yet, ironically, they strongly protested and sought to disqualify others who made the request of society that it *affirm* the value of preborn life.

Are citizens to be silenced because they belong to a church? Should not every person, every group, organization or denomination which truly believes that living human beings are being killed in abortion have the right to oppose this, even if it is approved by the law? Obviously, some would answer with an emphatic "no!" The familiarity of the expression ABORTION IS A CATHOLIC ISSUE prevents people from comprehending the scope of the idea. Not only is it a distortion of evidence and offensive in its appeals to latent Catholic bigotry, but it is also an affront to many denominations and individuals. It implies that only Roman Catholics have concern for the sanctity of life and the value and dignity of human beings.

Religion did not discover when life begins; biologists did. Religion did not establish that at the moment of conception a unique and separate individual exists; geneticists did. However, these scientific findings surely confirm that which has been revealed in God's Word: that human life is personal and precious to the Creator from its earliest beginning in the womb. That is why, if abortion is to be categorized, it is, indeed, a *catholic* issue! "Catholic," spelled with a small "c," means "universal"; that which "involves the interests of all." What could be more universal, more catholic in nature than the matter of human life?

Recalling the consistent opposition of God's people to abortion-on-demand, from Old Testament times through the present, one must wonder if it is not the prophetic witness itself which is under attack rather than the position of a specific denomination. A faithful prophet, speaking in the name of God, is never popular when the message is out of step with the culture it addresses. At such a time, all believers in traditional moral values will be unpopular. When the culture becomes evil enough, when the message of God through His people is attacked as immoral, the faithful witnesses become the unpatriotic ones, for they do not support the state; therefore, the religious institutions they represent are eventually viewed as the enemy of society.

Unpopularity appears to be the reward for those who choose the way of moral witness, those who confront a violent world with the force of truth. Yet far worse to consider than unpopularity are the implications of a coming World Judge, who is already here in the world. He is hidden, He told us, in the hungry, the thirsty, the outsider, the naked, the sick and the imprisoned. Could He be hidden in the unborn? Could Jesus himself be hidden in each fetal child who "came unto his own, and his own received him not"? [50]

9

But What About the Hard Cases— Rape? Abnormal Child?

It has been said that one can rouse the whole world over a single injustice, for the world can identify with one defenseless martyr. But when told of the numbers of unborn children who have been legally destroyed since the Supreme Court ruling of January 1973, society is intellectually disturbed but emotionally unmoved, for who can identify with almost nine million dead?

Such a number is beyond our comprehension and thus the reality of the situation is difficult to grasp. The sheer immensity of the abortion practice, the millions of dollars in profit which derive from the procedure and the vast structure of people involved in providing this service make for a network so entwined in the fabric of society that it becomes increasingly difficult to maintain critical and moral reflection. It is difficult to see little unborn human beings in what has become "big business." However, they are not the only ones who fade from view. Similarly blurred in the picture are those women and girls whose pregnancies create serious mental and emotional problems and are genuinely difficult.

It is realistic, accurate and humane to recognize that pregnancies exist which are distressful to the woman and her family. Unfortunately, because abortion-on-demand erodes a sense of collective responsibility for the woman in actual crisis, she is abandoned to heartless individualism. She is left alone with her own feelings and her own resources while isolated from positive solutions and support. In a society where programs, services and funding are geared toward abortion rather than toward addressing the causes which make a particular pregnancy a problem, the woman in stress is forsaken. Regardless of her personal desire to see the pregnancy to term, the social and economic pressures are often so great, that, in the absence of viable alternatives, such pressures become coercive toward abortion.

Perhaps the women most vulnerable to societal pressure are, first, those who are pregnant as a result of forcible rape and, secondly, those who have reason to believe that the child they are carrying has the potential for being physically or mentally disabled. To each of these situations we tend to bring great emotion and subjectivity. We project what we think we would do if it were our problem. Our advice is often based on how we would feel if we, or our wives or sisters, were the women involved. But *imagining* we are a rape victim, *imagining* we might deliver a child with defects, is not the same as being that woman in fact.

Thus, in a time of such great crisis, the pregnant woman is most vulnerable. We owe it to her to ask questions about the wisdom of abortion in her case. For her sake, because abortion is such an irreversible act, we need to take a closer look at such hard cases. We need to consider, in light of the trauma she has already experienced, whether abortion in these situations might hurt her more than help her. We need to be honest enough to consider that we as a society might have a selfish interest in promoting abortion under the guise of compassion for the woman.

RAPE

From whichever point of view experts approach this shameful and degrading crime, rape is still an enigma. While it is among the most feared acts of violence, it is, at the same time, one of the least understood. Justice for the victim and humane solutions to the problem remain elusive. One fact, however, is very clear: while the number of rape incidents have increased alarmingly, the conviction of rapists has the lowest rate of any violent crime.

Some state laws permitted abortion for rape long before the 1973 Supreme Court decision. It was, in fact, the first exception clause allowed for socio/economic reasons. The revulsion everyone feels at the crime of rape has led to a general attitude that abortion is the best way, if not the only way, to correct the problem of a resulting pregnancy.

Actually, pregnancy resulting from criminal rape is extremely rare. Several factors account for this, including the pure statistical odds against pregnancy resulting from any single act of intercourse. A study by the Guttmacher Institute found that the chances of pregnancy resulting from unprotected intercourse by two consenting *and* fertile adults was three percent. Further, rape studies have indicated a higher percentage of sterility and vasectomies among rapists. This factor plus the likelihood of infertility of women due either to their monthly cycle or the use of the pill, reduces the chances of pregnancy considerably. However, a major factor which makes the incidence of pregnancy from forcible rape almost nonexistent is that medical research indicates that women subjected to emotional trauma will not ovulate, even if under normal circumstances they would do so.[51]

Yet, consideration must be given to the needs, emotional and physical, of a woman who does become pregnant as a result of rape. The traumatic effects of the violence require that we provide her with the most sensitive and supportive counseling. It is, nevertheless, highly questionable to assume that the trauma of the assault itself and the subsequent pregnancy are best remedied by abortion. Psychiatrists indicate that it is impossible to predict for which woman an abortion would be more detrimental to her mental health than would be the strain of carrying the child to term. A raped woman's greatest needs when pregnancy occurs are for psychological counseling which meets her particular problems and the caring support of family and friends. Unfortunately, in the absence of these responses, abortion is viewed as the just course of action.

However, in essence, it is a solution with many similarities to that of the rape act itself. Every psychological profile of a rapist shows that his intent is to harm the woman. Rape is an act of aggression or violence, not of sex or lust. Is not harm to the unborn child the intent of the abortion procedure, one which is also an act of violence? Are not both rape and abortion the acts of a self-serving transgressor? What a rapist least wants is the woman herself. He does not see his victim as a person. Her body happens to be necessary to the solution or elimination of his personal problem. Do not the acts of rape and abortion both hold views of human beings which make objects of them? When a woman exercises her right to control her own body in total disregard of the body of another human being, it is called abortion. When a man acts out the same philosophy, it is called rape. We say that the rapist is sick for working out his problem by doing violence to an innocent human body. What then are we as a society when we say to the woman pregnant as a result of rape, "Now, you in turn solve your problem by doing violence to yet another innocent body."

For too long society has placed the blame on the woman victim of rape, implying that "she asked for it." In today's climate of heightened sensitivity, that myth is gradually being disspelled. Yet our outrage demands vengeance—someone must pay, and oddly enough, it is not the rapist but the innocent child who receives the sentence of capital punishment.

Does killing the child really help the raped

woman? Does killing the child really serve justice? Whose justice? St. Paul called the crucifixion a scandal because it offends our sense of justice. What made it an offense was that the innocent suffered for what the guilty have done. That is the mystery of the cross; the mystery of today is that our sense of justice is *not* offended when the innocent child is made to suffer for what the guilty have done. Yet, God, instructing His people in ways of mercy, said that "fathers shall not be put to death for the sins of their sons nor the sons for the sins of their fathers." [52]

The great gospel singer Ethel Waters revealed in her autobiography, *His Eye Is on the Sparrow*, that she was conceived following the rape of her 13-year-old mother. Was her value to society diminished by the circumstances surrounding her birth? The crime of the man who began her life in a repulsive act of violence, obviously, did not disqualify her from service in God's name.

Pregnancies which might occur from forcible rape can be prevented with immediate medical treatment given in the intervening hours between the sex act and the union of egg and sperm. However, if pregnancy does result, there are two victims, and both are innocent and both are in need of support. Abortion is a destructive approach to a human problem and involves the harmed and hurting woman in an aggressive action which cannot relieve the pain of the first tragedy. Rather than living with the memory of having destroyed the child developing within her, the victimized woman can be brought through a pregnancy which was not of her will by competent, supportive and loving care. Abortion may solve the emotional needs of a society repelled by rape, but does it really meet the needs of the two human beings most affected?

THE HANDICAPPED

There is a tribe in Africa which treats its infants born with grave deformities or those suffering from genetic irregularities as baby hippopotamuses. The members view such births as having accidentally occurred to humans and thus, labeling handicapped infants as animals, the appropriate action is clear. They gently place them in the river where hippopotamuses belong.[53]

What may seem like a pagan notion and a barbaric practice has been given a legitimate place in our civilization. The difference, however, is that we view those who do not meet our standards of perfection as vegetables instead of animals. In a 1973 issue of *Newsweek* magazine, the medical section carried an article entitled "Shall This Child Die?" [54] It reported on the work of Drs. Raymond S. Duff and A. G. M. Campbell at the Yale-New Haven Hospital. These men permit babies born with birth defects to die by deliberately withholding vital medical treatments. The doctors are convincing the parents that these children would be a financial burden and that they had "little or no hope of achieving meaningful 'humanhood.' " The doctors understood that they were breaking the law by doing away with what they called "vegetables," but they believed the law should be changed to allow for such deaths.

Sondra Diamond, who is in private practice as a

counseling psychologist and is currently completing her doctoral work, responded to the article in a letter to the editor of *Newsweek* which was published in the December 3, 1973, issue:

> I'll wager my entire root system and as much fertilizer as it would take to fill Yale University that you have never received a letter from a vegetable before this one, but much as I resent the term, I must confess that I fit the description of a "vegetable" as defined in the article, "Shall This Child Die?"
>
> Due to severe brain damage incurred at birth, I am unable to dress myself, toilet myself, or write; my secretary is typing this letter. Many thousands of dollars had to be spent on my rehabilitation and education in order for me to reach my present professional status as a counseling psychologist. My parents were also told, 35 years ago, that there was "little or no hope of achieving meaningful humanhood" for their daughter. Have I reached "humanhood"? Compared with Drs. Duff and Campbell I believe I have surpassed it!

Sondra Diamond's response focuses attention on our narrow understanding of what constitutes perfection and, therefore, value. She often asks an audience to consider the image distortion involved in our attitude towards those with motor or mental handicaps. "When a peach falls to the ground and is bruised, it is called a bruised peach," observes Sondra. "When a horse stumbles and is injured it is called an injured horse. Both retain their identity. But when people are bruised or injured we call them 'vegetables,' thereby changing their identity and allowing society to treat them as objects."

The technique of amniocentesis is increasingly being used to search out those in the womb whom some would call "vegetables." At approximately 16 weeks into pregnancy, a sample of fluid surrounding the child in the womb is removed with a needle. Extensive examination of the fluid can tell if what is in the womb is an "unsound fetus." The test does not, however, disclose the extent of the abnormality and has at times led to the death of children who, after an abortion, were discovered to be normal.

Is being different a reason for not being at all? How different does one have to be to be unacceptable? And who decides? In every age there are those who are able to convince themselves that they are superior to others and, therefore, entitled to dominate, enslave or exterminate the inferior ones. This elitist attitude pervades our society as well and is expressed in the abortion issue in a very subtle form. It is found in those who promote themselves as great humanitarians when they seek to alleviate the suffering of those diagnosed to be "unsound fetuses" by sparing them the ordeal of being born. For some the way to treat "vegetables" humanely is not to treat them as humans. Abortion is viewed as a compassionate correction to the "mistake" made by God.

Yet we cannot dehumanize others without becoming less human ourselves. The affirmation of the humanity of the unborn who are judged to be potentially handicapped or retarded will mean the affirmation of our own humanity. We who are "normals" are not greater than those with mental or motor disabilities. What is greater is our responsibility to respect and protect those who are differently gifted. God's words to Samuel are valid for us today: "Do not look at his appearance or at the height of his stature . . . for God sees not as man sees, for man looks at the outward appearance, but the Lord looks at the heart." [55]

The motor and mentally handicapped are not our problem; we are their problem. Those of us who may be "normal" physically and intellectually tend to overlook our own disabilities. It is our moral, emotional and spiritual handicaps which have created an "apartheid" society by giving privileges to those who are "perfect" and productive over those who are in one sense weak and unaccomplished. It is easy for us to accept each other when the other is just like us, but God calls us to "invite . . . the crippled, the lame, the blind, and you will be blessed, since they do not have the means to repay you." [56] Further, He asks, "Who made man's mouth? Or who makes him dumb or deaf, or seeing or blind? Is it not I, the Lord?" [57] Could it be that God has surprises hidden in those who are unlike us? Could it be that He intends them to stretch our narrow spirits, to help us grow in compassion and to teach us tolerance? Why are their handicaps unacceptable, while ours—those which are moral and spiritual—are ignored? Are the differences we judge to be strange, in reality simply "special"? Is destruction of such life the best our society can offer?

The elimination of the word "illegitimate" from birth certificates could make a significant difference in a raped woman's decision about the child she carries. Hospitalization policies which pay for the abortion of unwed women but not for delivery costs if she sees a pregnancy to term increase the economic burden of a rape victim. Adjustments in such health care plans could eliminate one form of coercion to abort. Insurance policies to cover newborns from birth would relieve the economic pressures confronting those who discover they are to be parents of a handicapped child. An immunization program which requires German measles vaccination for all grade school students would greatly diminish the potential for producing handicapped children, for it would decrease the risk of exposure by pregnant women to that disease. The provision of tax benefits and/or subsidies for people adopting handicapped children, the funding of community based care for the retarded and the provision of adequate maternal nutrition which affects the developing child could all contribute to a solution for THE HARD CASES, which would provide an alternative to abortion.

Can't we offer to the woman with a problem pregnancy more than the death of her child? Of course we can. The really hard question is: do we want to?

10

The Fallout

When the decision was made by the United States to drop the first atom bomb on Hiroshima in 1945, those responsible could predict with accuracy its immediate effects. However, only with the passage of time has the world been able to assess the varied kinds of fallout which have resulted from that explosion and which have proved to be more lasting and far-reaching than its initial radioactivity.

Who could have predicted the vast numbers of "habakusha," the "bomb people," who survived the explosion but have spent a lifetime dying? Who could have imagined that a whole generation later hospitals would exist primarily to treat the secondary effects of the bomb or that doctors would have entire practices devoted to patients whose lives have been immobilized by nightmares and severe depression? Who would have believed that the bomb which was "to compel peace" would lead thirty years later to the production of a "cleaner bomb," one designed to protect property while it destroys human lives?

The mushroom cloud of 1945 gave rise to the hope that civilization had finally reached the point where total war was no longer thinkable; but that was the hope of a generation which had not yet experienced the grim realities of the bomb's power and violence. That was the hope of a generation which had not faced the realities of future fallout.

When the decision was made by the United States Supreme Court in 1973 to override all current state anti-abortion statutes, it was viewed by many as a *legal* atom bomb. So sweeping and shattering, so disdaining of prior legal and moral tradition, so legislatively explosive was the ruling, that one of the dissenting justices was moved to describe it as "an exercise of raw judicial power." [58]

The immediate effects of the decision could be predicted with fair accuracy: the existing abortion laws of all fifty states were immediately struck down. Any woman could obtain an abortion during the first six months of pregnancy *without* a reason, and she could obtain an abortion in the last three months of pregnancy *with any reason* alleged to be detrimental to her life or health. A further immediate result was that it gave the United States the distinction of having the most permissive abortion law of any nation in the civilized world. However, it will be only with the passage of time that we will be able to assess the more lasting and far-reaching effects of that decision. But already the fallout has started.

Who could have imagined that, since the Supreme Court ruling, over one million legal abortions would be performed annually in this country or that abortions in numerous cities would outnumber live births?

> A change in abortion laws, from restrictive to permissive, appears—from *all data* and in *every country*—to bring forward a whole class of women who would otherwise not have wanted an abortion or felt the need for one. . . . Women can be conditioned (and are in many places) to want and feel the need for abortions. . . . Evidence from those countries where abortion-on-request has been long available (Russia, Japan, Hungary, for instance) shows that the subjectively-felt stress that leads women to seek an abortion is socially influenced.[59]

Who could have anticipated that the ruling, hailed by many as the one to settle once and for all the abortion controversy, would spawn still a second ruling which denied fathers the right to protect their unborn children from legal premature death?

In a subsequent 1976 case (*Planned Parenthood* v. *Danforth*) the Supreme Court ruled that a father need not give his consent or even be informed of the mother's decision to abort a child which together they had produced. Having in theory the right to beget children, a male has in actuality no rights which can be secured by law concerning the life of his fetal child. At a time when society is calling for greater responsibility on the part of fathers and greater involvement in the rearing of children, it seems ironic that the law would now deny them appropriate legal rights necessary to protect their children when they are most dependent and most vulnerable.

Historically, it has been noted that one of the features essential to the perpetuation of the slave system was the "denial of paternal relation." [60] Some of the most convincing arguments for the enactment of the Thirteenth Amendment were the arguments for the rights of slave fathers to their children, whether within or out of the womb. It was the aim of the men in Congress to protect the slave father in his "right of having a family, a wife, children, home" and to shield them from both the government and private individuals who would destroy them.

In 1976, Joseph Witherspoon, professor of law, testifying before the House of Representatives, emphasized the regression of rights which had occurred through the Supreme Court ruling. He referred to the purpose of the Thirteenth Amendment as it related to the restoration of the rights of a father while, in contrast, the 1976 Supreme Court ruling " . . . subjects the father of an unborn child to the uncontrolled discretion of its mother . . . (thereby) converting that father into a partial slave. . . . " [61]

Who could have foreseen the development of so negative a view of procreation that government doctors would describe unwanted pregnancy as "the second highest sexually transmitted disease" (with gonorrhea being number one)[62] or that an edition of the most widely read obstetrical text would refer to unwanted pregnancy as a "venereal disease." [63]

If one changes the terms, one can change the reality. What once was good becomes bad. What used to be called modesty is now called a "sex hang-up," chastity becomes "neurotic inhibition," and self-discipline is "unhealthy repression." Thus, the privilege of nurturing a new life, the gift of participating in human creation, is classified as a "venereal disease" while abortion becomes the curative treatment.

Medicine can be a manipulative tool. At a conference on pediatric research, a doctor commented on the influence of the attending physician. "I believe, as a physician . . . that I can persuade 99% of parents to my way of thinking if I really work at it, even if I am 100% wrong. If I tell them in such a way that I appear concerned and that I am knowledgeable . . . there is no question in my mind but that they will 'let me' cut off the infant's head." [64]

Pagan medical practitioners were involved in both healing and killing. These functions were separated by the Hippocratic Oath, in approximately 400 B.C., which articulated a new respect for life. In the ensuing generations, physicians who subscribed to that oath assumed the role of protective custodians for the unborn. Committing themselves only to healing, they swore "not to give a woman an abortifacient pessary." That oath, which formed the foundation for civilized medicine for 1500 years, is no longer required of graduating medical students. The Supreme Court ruling of 1973 further has entangled medicine in a regressive process by once again allowing the physician to be both healer and exterminator.

Who would have anticipated that abortion would be used increasingly to end the lives of healthy unborn infants simply because they are female?

Parents making an abortion decision are sometimes using a technique called amniocentesis, originally developed to detect and treat RH factor problems before birth, for purposes of sex selection. In a world where male children generally are preferred, unborn female children are experiencing the ultimate in discrimination. "Of almost 100 pregnant women recently tested and told the sex of their unborn children, a female fetus was detected in 46. Twenty-nine of these mothers elected to abort. Of 53 found to be carrying males, only 1 woman chose to terminate her pregnancy." [65] Fifty-two males but only 17 females survived the sex screening.

Newer, quicker, easier and earlier methods for determining sex are expected within a short time. With simple tests easily available and with half the American women who want children preferring boys (according to a 1977 study of the University of Michigan published in a journal of Planned Parenthood), what will be the effect on society when the male-female balance is disrupted? What kind of world results when society is male-dominated? What happens to women's rights, equality and value when to be a female is to be genetically defective?

To what degree these and related changes will affect the role of medicine, the health of women, the parent-child relationship, marriage, the family, the economy and the psyche of our society would be conjecture at this point. What is certain, however, is that the human and societal fallout from abortion-on-demand is a reality which we all must live, not only those who are directly involved. "You must not only want what you want," says a French proverb, "but you must want what it leads to."

The mushroom cloud of Hiroshima continues to distort and affect lives today, although its initial impact was experienced over thirty years ago. In 1978 newspapers carried a story entitled "Witnesses to Atomic Tests Tell of Years of Poor Health." A number of men, testifying from wheelchairs and on crutches, told members of Congress of the severe illnesses which had plagued them as a result of having had some contact with the atom bomb. Sterility, serious blood conditions, physical impairment and leukemia were but a few of the effects experienced by these workers. While not primary victims of the bomb, these men, exposed to it in some way, eventually became secondary victims. Newspapers that same year also carried stories of the high incidence of cancer found among people in Utah who "used to get up early to watch the brilliant pre-dawn flashes and enormous mushroom clouds 100 miles away." [66] The toll of victims mounts: those who died in the explosion, those who were at the death scene but survived, those who helped produce the destruction, and even those who stood at a distance and watched.

Is it possible that there are further victims of abortion-on-demand, not merely those who can be recorded statistically at over one million aborted dead each year? Perhaps, also, victims are those who participate in the killing in some way—through tax monies, counseling, apathy or silence. Perhaps, as the fallout settles, we, too, will discover that those who quietly stand by and watch are victims. We, like the "habakusha," survived the destruction but spend lifetimes dying. It is we who must go on living, having exposed our hearts and minds, our children and society to the fallout from a pragmatic ethic which deems as "good" that which destroys, hails as curative that which kills.

11

The Choice

"An imbecile habit" was the way G. K. Chesterton described the contemporary view which believes that a creed held in one age cannot be held in another. What was credible in the twelfth century, such a view maintains, is not credible in the technological twentieth century. In contradiction Chesterton argued:

> You might as well say that a certain philosophy can be believed Mondays, but cannot be believed on Tuesdays. You might as well say of a view of the cosmos that it was suitable to half-past three, but not suitable to half-past four. What a man can believe depends on his philosophy, not on the clock or the century. If a man believes in an unalterable natural law, he cannot believe in any miracle in any age. If a man believes in a will behind law, he can believe in

> any miracle in any age. . . . Therefore in dealing
> with any historical answer, the point is not whether
> it was given in our time, but whether it was given in
> answer to our question." [67]

But what *is* our question? To abort or not to abort?
To allow for infanticide or euthanasia? To embark on
genetic engineering or test-tube fertilization? No,
none of these is the question. As man seemingly becomes an endangered species, as manipulative tech-
nology considers the "improvement" of the human
race, the fundamental and most serious question of
this century is: *What does it mean to be human?*

Who will answer our question? Can the church,
when so many of its leaders have already capitulated
to the "imbecile habit" of maintaining that what was
relevant in Christ's age is not relevant in ours? How
strange in light of the statement by Malachi Martin,
church scholar and historian, who observed that while
some obvious differences exist between the first and
the twentieth century, never before has Christianity
been in a world as similar to the one in which it was
born. Because of this likeness, his article in the *National Review* urged Christian theologians and
teachers to turn back to the rich resources found in
traditional biblical teachings and focus "the old, in-
fallible light" upon the problems of today's world.

Yet that is precisely the problem! It is an *old* light.
In our throw-away society old ideas, as old people,
lack value. Unlike coins and stamps which are en-
hanced by age, old solutions do not become collectors'
items. While many things *have* value simply because
they are old, the Ten Commandments, for instance,
have been devalued in this century on precisely these

same grounds.

In light of what faces us—the fundamental question about the humanity of man and the monumental problems of the future of man—there is an essential need for a clear statement of values. But can those who cherish enduring values and time-honored standards make a clear statement, when so many of them, in absorbing the helplessness and hopelessness of the world, have retreated from their responsibilities as citizens? "The world is so evil that it must be about to end. Why bother making repairs on a sinking ship? Besides, nothing can be changed." Edmund Burke, a Christian statesman, said long ago, "All that is necessary for the triumph of evil is that good men do nothing." Evil, suffering, violence—all these are bad in a society. But what is far worse is becoming "used to it," tolerating and "learning to live with it." Then apathy becomes terribly appealing; withdrawal becomes frightfully enticing; silence becomes awfully tempting. We become as the crowd around the cross at Golgotha. We recognize the injustice, we see the suffering of the innocent and abhor the violence of the act, but like those on the day of Christ's crucifixion, we do nothing. "Sitting down, they watched him there." [68] Spectators. Bystanders. Onlookers. But, thank God, something else—witnesses!

There were some there who understood the significance of what they saw and who then made a clear statement, so that you and I, two thousand years later, can perceive what they saw at the cross. We see that, then as now, man's solution to a problem is the destruction of the innocent and that man's justice is conditioned by what is socially expedient. Yet, most important, there at the cross we were given a new way, a better way, *the Way*. It is there that we can find the answer to our question, for it is there that we were given a choice. The great tragedy of today, though, is that so many seem unaware that there is a choice. We can say that "everybody's doing it," but there are countless numbers who have chosen *not* to do it. We can say, "When in Rome do as the Romans do," but there are untold numbers who do not think that what the Romans are doing ought to be done and have chosen *not* to do it.

In Eugene Ionesco's play called "Rhinoceros," a human character turns into a rhinoceros. That same transformation is undergone by all but one of the human beings as the play progresses. The heroine, who witnesses a man turning into an animal, provides the key to the drama's message. "Just before he became a beast," she says, "his last human words were, 'We must move with the times.' "

With our very humanity at stake, the people following the Jesus Way must sound the warning to our generation that to "move with the times" may make life more efficient, more technological and productive, but it will eventually make life less human and less humane. There is a choice, and we need to proclaim it while there is still time.

The choice to be made is between two diametrically opposed philosophies which cannot co-exist, for the adoption of one inevitably destroys the other. On the one hand, there is the choice of the Judeo-Christian ethic which accords value and dignity to every human life regardless of age and condition. It is an ethic which recognizes that every human life is created by and in the image of God. On the other hand is secular humanism in which man is not viewed as someone special or set apart. He is merely "the naked Ape," an improved animal. What man wants should be determined by himself alone, for man is under obligation to no one but himself. If God is acknowledged at all, the humanist adopts the position that He is either irrelevant or dead.

Leo Pfeffer, a well-known lawyer who has testified in support of the 1973 Supreme Court abortion decision, has also been influential in achieving court decisions which have interpreted the First Amendment so narrowly as to all but banish religion from public life. Thus, his 1977 article entitled "Issues That Divide: The Triumph of Secular Humanism," [69] should be of special interest to those with concern for preserving values. Citing instances such as tax aid to religious schools, prayer in public schools, sexual behavior in general, divorce and abortion, he indicates that in each case over the past several decades any distinctively religious position has been systematically abandoned by American society in favor of nonreligious alternatives which comprise secular humanism. He notes that the churches have little public influence, and he sees each case as a defeat for the churches and a triumph for their philosophical enemies. The church is losing a fighting battle, in Pfeffer's opinion, and he views abortion as the last stand. Even on this, he believes, the church will eventually give in.

Those, like Pfeffer, who see no role for religion in American life except in a purely private capacity have long been aware of how crucial the abortion issue is to the demise of the Judeo-Christian ethic. They have not hidden their intent and, indeed, made it very clear in the Humanist Manifesto II, published a few months after the Supreme Court decision in 1973, which supports the right to abortion. Some Christians optimistically view recent developments as the healthy fruits of pluralism, in which all points of view are accommodated. They fail to understand, however, that secular humanism views the Christian faith itself as "harmful." Not to be accommodated are those religions which the Humanist Manifesto describes as "dogmatic and authoritarian." Humanists believe that those with "faith in the prayer-hearing God, who is assumed to love and care for persons . . . do a disservice to the human species." [70]

That such beliefs constitute for some an "outmoded faith" was also emphasized in a 1970 statement which appeared in the official journal of the California Medical Association. The editorial, supporting abortion-on-demand, clearly indicated that the battle lines have been sharply drawn. An examination of numerous excerpts from that article, which was titled "A New Ethic for Medicine and Society," [71] will serve to further establish the choice with which society is confronted.

> The traditional Western ethic has always placed great emphasis on the intrinsic worth and equal value of every human life regardless of its stage or condition. This ethic . . . has been the basis for most of our laws and much of our social policy. The reverence for each and every human life has also been a keystone of Western medicine.[72]

"The traditional," the *old* ethic, was the foundation upon which was built humane social policy, a just system of law and compassionate treatment for the sick and dying. In "moving with the times," however, the author calls for "A New Ethic," which, the editorial acknowledges,

> is quite distinctly at variance with the Judeo-Christian ethic and carries serious philosophical, social, economic and political implications for Western society and perhaps for the world society.

> It will become necessary and acceptable to place relative rather than absolute values on such things as human lives. . . .

> The process of eroding the old ethic and substituting the new has already begun. It may be seen most clearly in changing attitudes toward human abortion. In defiance of the long-held Western ethic of intrinsic and equal value for every human life regardless of its stage, condition or status, abortion is becoming accepted by society as morally right and even necessary.[73]

Abortion is the cutting edge, the initial wedge, for the new ethic. It is the tip of the iceberg in the proposed revision of what it means to be human. Despite all the rhetoric about abortion being a matter of private morality, it has far-reaching public implications. If what we are interested in is a stop-gap measure, then abortion seems reasonable. If what we desire are results, then abortion seems like an answer. But it is an option which does not exist in a vacuum, for it involves the sacrifice of not only the unborn child, but a way of life, an entire ethic. As the seamless robe of Christ, to unloose but one thread of its fabric is to eventually unloose it all.

One may anticipate further developments . . . as the

problems of birth control and birth selection are extended *inevitably* [emphasis mine] to death selection and death control whether by the individual or by society.[74]

In the acceptance of abortion-on-demand, there occurs a subtle but profound shift in the attitude of society toward all people who are unwanted, imperfect and dependent. The same forces involved in legalizing abortion, while claiming to alleviate the suffering of a woman with an unwanted pregnancy, are the same forces involved in the promotion of infanticide and euthanasia, claiming to want to eliminate the suffering of the handicapped, sick and senile. When we choose to offer death as an alternative to suffering, the list of those who qualify under the "new ethic" expands greatly.

It is worth noting that this shift in public attitudes has affected the church . . . rather than the reverse.[75]

Mark Twain once said, "Its name is Public Opinion. It is held in reverence. It settles everything. Some think it is the voice of God." The church, instead of acting, is being acted upon. Public opinion increasingly shapes its witness and molds its ministry. The church has become the rear guard instead of the vanguard. The Christian, instead of serving as a pilot, leading the way, has become a Pilate, the classic example of a man who did not want to get involved. Pathetic Pilate, unwilling to do what was wrong—condemn the Innocent to death—was also unwilling to do what was right—to use his voice to save Him who was condemned. So he washed his hands of the whole matter and chose personal immunity over public responsibility.[76]

As the editorial indicates, such "hand washing" is fostered in the abortion issue by the use of deceptive language.

> Since the old ethic has not yet been fully displaced it has been necessary to separate the idea of abortion from the idea of killing, which continues to be socially abhorrent.

> The result has been a curious avoidance of the scientific fact, which everyone really knows, that human life begins at conception and is continuous whether intra-uterine or extra-uterine until death.

> The very considerable semantic gymnastics which are required to rationalize abortion as anything but taking a human life would be ludicrous if they were not often put forth under socially impeccable auspices. It is suggested that this schizophrenic sort of subterfuge is necessary because while a new ethic is being accepted the old has not yet been rejected.[77]

A number of years have passed since the publication of that article. Volumes have been written in support of the new ethic. The Supreme Court abortion rulings are evidence of the effectiveness of "semantic gymnastics." The massive abortion business demonstrates the success of the "schizophrenic subterfuge." But the millions of unborn children who have violently and legally died tell another story. It is a sad story, for it could not have happened without our silence. It would not exist without our apathy, and it could not continue without our indifference. We may no longer ask, "How can they do such a thing?" By our inaction, we have become "they."

A certain man went down from Jerusalem to Jericho,

and fell among thieves, who stripped him of his raiment, and wounded him, and departed, leaving him half dead.

And by chance there came down a certain priest that way and when he saw him, perhaps he thought, "Well, I wouldn't rob a traveller myself, but I support the right of others to choose," for he passed by on the other side.

And likewise a Levite, when he was at that place, came and looked on him, but perhaps he thought, "Every man should be a wanted man, and obviously this one wasn't," for he, too, passed by on the other side.

But a certain Samaritan, as he journeyed, came where he was; and when he saw him, he had compassion on him and history has forever called him "good." But not until he had set aside his plans and his schedule for another; not until he had sacrificed his time and treasure for one in need; not until he had risked his own safety and, perhaps, even his life in trying to save the helpless.

Abortion is not the solution to a problem; it is the elimination of a human being perceived to be the problem. It is an action which calls us to embrace the superficial rather than the sacrificial, for abortion costs us little in terms of self-denial, self-sacrifice and servanthood. That it is a callous, cruel and brutal way of handling human life is implied in the stunned question of the small child, "Who broke the baby?"

It was not an easy question to answer then nor is it easy to answer now, for "who" includes so many of us. Not just the aborting mother or the abortionist, but all of us who are silent and apathetic, those who "sit-

ting down . . . watched"; all of us who are unrespon-
sive and uninvolved, those who "pass by on the other
side." "Who" includes all of us whose inaction contra-
dicts our beliefs as Christians, whose lethargy discred-
its our convictions as Americans, whose inertia disaf-
firms our commitment to the Judeo-Christian ethic.
We, too, are the guilty bystanders who also "broke the
baby."

Notes

1. On January 22, 1973, the United States Supreme Court in two separate decisions (*Roe* v. *Wade* and *Doe* v. *Bolton*) ruled that all state laws relating to abortion would have to meet the following guidelines:

   In the first trimester, the first three months of pregnancy, the state must leave the abortion decision entirely to the woman, who was to make the decision in consultation with a physician.

   In the second trimester, approximately the fourth through the sixth month of pregnancy, the state may, if it chooses, regulate abortion in ways "reasonably related to maternal health." That is, the state may establish who is permitted to do abortions and where they are to take place. The state may not, however, enact laws which would prevent the unborn from being aborted during this trimester.

In the third trimester, approximately the seventh month through birth, the law may prohibit a woman from having an abortion unless it is necessary to preserve her "life or health." However, since the court defined the word "health" in a sense so broad as to encompass even her preferred life-style and social well-being, it is virtually impossible for a state to protect the unborn until the moment of birth.

2. Luke 10:30-33, KJV.
3. 2 Timothy 1:13, 14.
4. This must be understood in the paradox of Christian liberation. We are freed to become slaves of others (Matt. 20:26, 27). Enslavement to Christ produces liberation for the Christian. Christ liberates us from ourselves, our self-centeredness and selfishness. He frees us to introduce self-discipline into our lives, self-sacrifice in choices and self-control in our behavior. He liberates us to place ourselves under His control for service to others.
5. *Philadelphia Inquirer,* April 4, 1976, p. 4C.
6. Genesis 3:5, 6.
7. Romans 12:1, Amplified New Testament.
8. Romans 10:14, paraphrased.
9. Isaiah 44:2; Psalm 139:13.
10. Luke 1:41-44.
11. Pride, covetousness, anger, envy, gluttony, laziness, lust.

12. 1 Peter 1:8; 1 John 4:20.
13. Romans 5:10.
14. Pamela Zekman and Pamela Warrick, The Phil Donahue Show, January 1979.
15. Luke 1:30-35.
16. The Koine Greek, the most precise form of language communication ever to exist, had a variety of words to describe the different growth periods of children. *Brephos* suffices to speak of the unborn as well as those in childhood who "hast known the holy scriptures which are able to make thee wise unto salvation through faith which is in Christ Jesus" (2 Tim. 3:15). We must conclude that the usage of this word by the scripture writers under the guidance of the Holy Spirit implies that a child is a child whether preborn or newborn.
17. Luke 1:41, 44.
18. Luke 2:12, 16.
19. Luke 18:15.
20. The word "conceptus" is occasionally used to identify unborn children from the moment of their conception until approximately 14 days later. More common is the word "embryo," generally used to denote the child until the eighth week after conception. Beginning in the third month until birth, the child is identified by the term "fetus."
21. Prof. A. W. Liley, excerpted from a speech delivered on November 18, 1970, entitled "The Termination of Pregnancy or the Extermination of the Fetus."
22. Philippians 1:9, 10. Good News for Modern Man.
23. *Planned Parenthood of Central Missouri* v. *Dan-*

forth, July 1, 1976.

24. Deuteronomy 30:19.
25. The "right to privacy" is not mentioned in the U.S. Constitution. The Supreme Court in 1973 was not sure where that right was located. "We feel," said Justice Blackmun, "that the right is located in the Fourteenth Amendment. . . . " But he said it might also be in the Ninth Amendment. He indicated in the ruling that the exact constitutional provision for such a right was vague.
26. Isaiah 49:1, 5.
27. Jeremiah 1:5.
28. Galatians 1:15.
29. Jerusalem Bible translation.
30. "A Government-run Opium Factory," *LIFE*, June 25, 1971, p. 5.
31. E. Hines Zimmerman, "Abortion Is Nothing New," *Applied Christianity,* October 1973, pp. 5-8.
32. "Shoplifters, Beware," *Reader's Digest,* reprint of Pittsburgh Press article of September 10, 1972, pp. 179-184.
33. Christopher Tietze, M.D., "Abortion in Europe," Annual Meeting of the American Public Health Association, San Francisco, October 1966.
34. H. Frederiksen and James Brackett, "Demographic Effects of Abortion," U.S. Public Health Reports, December 1966.
35. Jill Knight, member of Parliament, *Birmingham Evening Mail and Dispatch,* Birmingham, England, October 15, 1966.
36. E. N. Akers, Director Colorado Health Department, Denver Associated Press Report, January 13, 1970.

37. Milton Halpern, Chief Medical Examiner, New York, *Daily News,* February 20, 1971.
38. 1 Thessalonians 5:21.
39. "Risky Abortions," *TIME,* November 27, 1978, p. 52.
40. "A Prospective Study of the Effects of Induced Abortion on Subsequent Reproductive Function," Department of Health, Education and Welfare, National Institute of Child Health and Human Development, Summary of Progress, September 1, 1975-May 31, 1978.
41. "Risky Abortions," *op. cit.*
42. "Report on Criminal Abortion," submitted by the American Medical Association Committee on Criminal Abortion at the Twelfth Annual Meeting of the AMA, Louisville, Kentucky, May, 1859, David Keyser, researcher.
43. *Ibid.*
44. Senator Jesse Helms of North Carolina; Representative Henry Hyde of Illinois, 1978.
45. "Ecumenical War over Abortion," *TIME,* January 29, 1979, pp. 62, 63.
46. William F. Gavin, "An Open Letter to Walter Cronkite," *Human Events,* March 11, 1978, p. 196.
47. "Abortion in Japan after 25 Years," *Medical World News,* November 9, 1973, p. 37.
48. Harold B. Kuhn, "Caring for the Caretakers," *Christianity Today,* August 12, 1977, p. 41.
49. "A Call for Concern" appeared as a paid advertisement in *The Christian Century,* October 12, 1977.
50. John 1:11.

51. F. D. Mecklenburg, M.D., "Indications for Induced Abortion," *Abortion and Social Justice,* New York, 1972.
52. Deuteronomy 24:16.
53. Paul Ramsey, "Protecting the Unborn," *Child and Family,* 1978, p. 3.
54. "Shall This Child Die?" *NEWSWEEK,* Medical Section, November 12, 1973.
55. 1 Samuel 16:7.
56. Luke 14:13, 14.
57. Exodus 4:11.
58. Mr. Justice White, United States Supreme Court, dissenting opinion, January 22, 1973.
59. Abortion: Thinking and Experiencing, Daniel Callahan, Director of the Institute of Society, Ethics and the Life Sciences, *Christianity and Crisis,* January 8, 1973, p. 296.
60. Senator Charles Sumner of Massachusetts, a framer of the Thirteenth Amendment.
61. Joseph P. Witherspoon, Professor of Law, University of Texas, testimony before the House of Representatives, Sub-Committee on Civil and Constitutional Rights, February 4, 1976.
62. "Abortion as a Treatment for Unwanted Pregnancy: the Number Two Sexually Transmitted Disease," a paper presented by three physicians from the United States Center for Disease Control before an annual convention of Planned Parenthood Physicians, 1976.
63. *Williams Obstetrics,* Fifteenth Edition, p. 842.
64. "Ethical Dilemmas in Current Obstetric and Newborn Care," Ross Conference on Pediatric Research, Columbus, Ohio, October 1973.

65. *Medical World News,* December 1, 1975, p. 45.
66. "Mushroom Clouds Blamed for Sprouting Cancers," *Philadelphia Inquirer,* November 11, 1978.
67. G. K. Chesterton, *ORTHODOXY,* 1908.
68. Matthew 27:36.
69. Leo Pfeffer, "Issues That Divide: The Triumph of Secular Humanism," Journal of Church and State, Spring, 1977.
70. Humanist Manifesto II, August 1973.
71. "A New Ethic for Medicine and Society," *CALIFORNIA MEDICINE,* Official Journal of the California Medical Association, September, 1970, Volume 113, Number 3.
72. *Ibid.*
73. *Ibid.*
74. *Ibid.*
75. *Ibid.*
76. Matthew 27:24.
77. *Op. cit.*